REVEILLE

for

RADICALS

REVEILLE

for

RADICALS

SAUL D. ALINSKY

> Let them call me rebel and welcome,
> I feel no concern from it; but I
> should suffer the misery of devils,
> were I to make a whore of my
> soul. . . .
>
> THOMAS PAINE

Vintage Books

A Division of Random House

NEW YORK

To the memory of Helene

Contents

Introduction to the Vintage Edition

A GENERATION has passed since I wrote *Reveille for Radicals*. Reading it after all that time was an eerie, schizy experience. The angry, defiant, go-for-broke, irreverent youngster coming through in these pages seemed almost but not quite another person. At times I found myself saying to him, "Cool it, kid, you're taking on a thousand-to-one odds as though it were an even bet; you'll learn when you get more experience to watch it—if the odds are higher than a hundred to one."

I began to write, "As I look back upon my youth . . ." but the words stick, for I don't feel an hour or year older. I guess that when you are constantly in the arena of conflict, you just don't have the time to grow older. Life is conflict and in conflict you're alive; action does not admit age into the arena. Sudden death, yes; but gradual age, no.

As I look at *Reveille* after twenty years of more experience in many different battlefields, cities, with many different peoples, issues, religious institutions and against many different opponents, the question naturally comes up as to what I would change if I were writing *Reveille* today. For me, the question can't be separated from another: "Have I changed and, if so, how?" Of course I have changed. It is idiocy to assume that anyone can be alive and not be changing constantly. There are many who go through the years without changing but they are the ones who huddle on a chronological treadmill searching for an illusionary security and something called status. The senility of security and status even afflicts many of the so-called young. They never live. Life is an adventure of passion, risk, danger, laughter, beauty, love, a burning curiosity to go with the action to see what it is all about, to search for a pattern of meaning, to burn one's bridges because you're never going to go back anyway, and to live to the end. Terrified by this dramatic vista, most people just exist; they turn from the turbulence of change and try to hide in their private make-believe harbors, called in politics conservatism; in the church, prudence; and in everyday life, being sensible.

It is in chronological youth when time ahead seems endless that one is tempted to take a chance and live —particularly so if one's youth takes place, as did mine, in a period of upheaval and massive dramatic change, with the collapse of many accepted values and the opening up of an uncharted future, offering the beckoning adventure of the search for the new life. The accepted values of security, work, and money as the way to "happiness" went in the great crash of 1929. In the crisis, life became polarized and good and evil stood clear and unmistakable.

The years of the 1930's followed, when I was in my twenties. Days of the great depression, F.D.R.'s New Deal, John L. Lewis' organized labor revolution of the C.I.O. battling the corporate giants of America; times of compassion which found those in the North and East suffering with the plight of the sharecroppers and Okies of the South and Midwest. A time when black and white moved together in their need for strength in face of the common enemy of unemployment and low wages; the great depression heightened man's awareness and concern for his fellow man. This and more of the same was happening at home while abroad Europe was boiling up a Wagnerian devil's brew of unbelievable madness in the twilight of civilization.

The pillars of the past had become tombstones and those which survived were suspect and challenged. Disillusionment's child is irreverence, and irreverence became one of my major heritages from an angry, irreverent generation. In this way, I have not changed. I am still irreverent. I still feel the same contempt for and still reject so-called objective decisions made without passion and anger. Objectivity, like the claim that one is nonpartisan or reasonable, is usually a defensive posture used by those who fear involvement in the passions, partisanships, conflicts, and changes that make up life; they fear life. An "objective" decision is generally lifeless. It is academic and the word "academic" is a synonym for irrelevant.

I have changed in that I have learned to freeze my hot anger into cool anger and to make my intuitive irreverence conscious, to challenge not only the opposition but myself, to realize and accept the prime importance of the Socratic adage about the unexamined life. Through action, reflection, study, testing, and synthesis I have learned to distill *experience* from living. Experience is the integrating of the actions and events of life so that they arrange themselves into meaningful universal patterns. Most people distill or digest this product of experience from the actions and events of their daily lives, so that much of it passes through their intellectual systems as segmented happenings and separate memories. I have learned to search for laws of change, to discover for myself such simple truths as that the real action is in the reaction. These and other lessons of the past are the basis for my forthcoming book, *Rules for Revolution*, which I am now completing. In short, cool anger and conscious understanding based on experience have made my actions far more calculated, deliberate, directive, and effective. Now my actions are designed primarily to induce certain reactions based on an analysis of circumstances. I have learned not to confuse power patterns with the personalities of the individuals involved; in other words, to hate conditions, not individuals. Thus I have learned to become in many ways the master rather than the servant of my tactics, and to develop far more effective tactics—economic, political, and social—than the simple, hot, angry, personalized denunciation. One must learn to see one's opponent in the context of circumstances to which one must respond. Understanding these forces enables one to develop the strategy which my opponents describe as Alinsky-style mass ju-jitsu. The opposition is always stronger than you are and so his own strength must be used against him. I have repeatedly said that the status quo is your best ally if properly goaded and guided. I have also learned to avoid succumbing to a rationale which would permit me the escape of becoming a rhetorical radical and not a radical realist. These are a few of the lessons learned from continuous action since I wrote *Reveille for Radicals.*

Through experience you learn to see people not as sellouts and betrayers of moral principles, but as the result of ongoing processes. In the past I attacked labor leaders who started out lean, hungry, and idealistic and as they succeeded became fat-bellied, fat-headed, and cynical. I now see these people as having moved from the *Have-Not's* to the *Have's*, and that morality is largely a rationalization of the point you happen to occupy in the power pattern at a given time. If you're a *Have-Not* you're out *to get*, and your morality is an appeal to a law higher than man-made laws —the noblest ideals of justice and equality. When you become a *Have* then you are out *to keep* and your morality is one of law, order, and the rights of property over other rights.

A clear example of this is the story of what happened to a major organization in what was at one time the worst of America's slums, Chicago's notorious

Back of the Yards, the site of Upton Sinclair's *The Jungle*.

In the dawn of the Back of the Yards the members—mostly Polish-Americans—fought discrimination against themselves, and to justify their cause they had to be men and denounce all discrimination against anyone. Then they stood and fought as the David of equality for all mankind against the Goliath of prejudice, segregation, and the repression of the prevailing *Have's.*° Through the years they mounted victory upon victory and moved steadily up the ladder from the *Have-Not's* to the *Have-a-Little-and-Want-More's.*

They then cast their lot with the *Have's,* as—with a few burning individual exceptions—the middle class always does. They moved into the nightfall of success, and the dreams of achievement which make men fight were replaced by the restless nightmares of fear: fear of change, fear of losing material possessions. Today they are part of the city's establishment and are desperately trying to keep their community unchanged. They rationalize thus: they are not trying to keep blacks out but rather are trying to keep their people in. They are segregationists. They have experienced the fate of all successful organizations of men: witness the Christian Church as it evolved from the days of the martyrs to what it is today, organized labor from

° It was because of their position at the time that Adlai E. Stevenson, Governor of Illinois, wrote the Back of the Yards Council on April 23, 1951:

If I were asked to choose in all America a single agency which I felt most admirably represented all that our democracy stands for, whose aims most faithfully reflected our ideals of brotherhood, tolerance, charity, and the dignity of the individual, I would select the Back of the Yards Council. All that you have done for the health, the social welfare, the economic advancement, and the spiritual and temporal happiness of the people in your community is to me one of the most heartening accomplishments in community relations in our time. I only wish we had more such organizations, doing more of the kind of social work the Council is carrying on so well.

the days of rebellion to what it is today, and so with all victorious revolutionary movements that trade in their birthrights for a mess of property, power and the grand illusion of security.

Do I regret my leadership in organizing the Back of the Yards? I do not. If I could have foreseen what has come to pass I would still do it again because of the many changes that have at the same time come about in some 200,000 lives in what had been a jungle of despair and defeat.

The passing years have not brought disillusionment but, on the contrary, a firmer and deeper faith in people and the principles stated in *Reveille for Radicals*. This is the result of my having learned more about the world as it is and more about not confusing it with the world as I would like it to be. To understand the behavior of people as they are in the real world precludes either disillusionment or cynicism. You learn to be realistic in your expectations. You go on using the probables in the eternal struggle to achieve the improbable.

This brings me to the question I have been confronted with everywhere: "What, if anything, is your ideology?" Here we come to grips with a basic issue. What kind of ideology, if any, can an organizer have in a free society, working for a free society? The prerequisite for an ideology is possession of a basic truth. For example, a Marxist begins with his prime truth that all evils are caused by the exploitation of the proletariat by the capitalists. From this evolves the idea of the revolution to end capitalism, then the premise of reorganization into a new social order or the dictatorship of the proletariat, and finally the last stage—the political paradise of communism. The Christians also have a prime truth: the divinity of Christ and the tripartite nature of God. Once these concepts are accepted, a formula for a way of life follows step by step.

A free man working for an open society is in a serious dilemma. To begin with, he does not have a fixed truth. Truth to him is relative and changing. He accepts the late Justice Learned Hand's statement that "the mark of a free man is that ever-gnawing inner uncertainty as to whether or not he is right." Having no fixed truth he has no final answers, no dogma, no formula, no panacea. The consequence is that he is ever on the hunt for the causes of man's plight and the general propositions that help to make sense out of man's irrational world. He is constantly examining life, including his own, to get some idea of what it means.

The banner of the free-society organizer emphasizes the question mark. He challenges and tests his own beliefs and findings. Irreverence again becomes important because it is essential to questioning. Curiosity become compulsive. His most common word is "Why?"

Another factor that blocks the organizer in a free society from adopting a fixed ideology is that ideologies are primarily rooted in the laws of cause and effect. Once you know the cause and deal with it, then certain effects will ensue. The organizer for a free society, however, shares the view of quantum physics which subordinates cause and effects to probability. If probability is at the heart of modern physics, then it is also at the heart of social mechanics. It is impossible to have a closed ideological system based on probabilities. An ideology, a dogma, demands certainty, not probability.

An organizer for a free society must be a creative person; his search for universals means the fulfillment of the highest goals of a creative mind—the finding of similarities in seemingly different or dissimilar things in our world. It is only in the discovery of these similarities that we have hope for even dimly understanding what we call life. Only with these similarities can we begin to construct natural laws of politics and detect an order in much of the chaos and carnage about us.

Does this then mean that the organizer in a free society for a free society is rudderless? I believe that the organizer in and for a free society has a far better sense of direction and compass than the closed-society organizer with his proscribed political ideology.

First, the free-society organizer is loose, resilient, fluid, and on the move in a society which is in a state of extraordinary and constant change. He is not shackled with a dogma. In our world today rigidity is fatal. The free-society organizer is constantly growing and learning. He knows and accepts political relativity.

In the end he has one all-consuming conviction, one belief, one article of faith—a belief in people, a complete commitment to the belief that if people have the power, the opportunity to act, in the long run they will, most of the time, reach the right decisions. The alternatives to this would be rule by the elite—either dictatorship or a political aristocracy of some form. I am not concerned if this faith in people is regarded as a prime truth and a contradiction to what I have already written, for life is a story of contradictions.

Believing in people, the radical has the job of organizing people so that they will have the power and opportunity to best meet each unforeseeable future crisis as they move ahead to realize those values of equality, justice, freedom, the preciousness of human life, and all those rights and values propounded by Judeo-Christianity and democratic tradition. Democracy is not an end but the best means toward achieving these values. These values are not even debatable in a free society; they are accepted, they are the reasons for the democratic society. They cannot be placed on the ballot; no state has the right to vote segregation or any other violation of these values. If the democratic process is used to subvert freedom then the process prostitutes the purpose of an open society and democracy is dead. Here there can be no compromise. Earlier I said that my irreverence changed from intuitive to conscious. All radicals acting for change must attack the sacred cows of the past and many of the present. These sacred cows are accepted as terminal truths and serve as the supporting rationale for the ways of the past. *A scared human being gives birth to a sacred cow.* Since the genesis and survival of sacred cows is rooted in fear and reverence, it follows that those who want change must be against sacred cows and not only innately irreverent but outwardly, purposefully irreverent in their actions. They must be iconoclastic bulldozers willing to be regarded as profane spoilers of the sacred myths.

Irreverence is essentially profane. Originally one was profane by taking the Lord's name in vain. When one challenges or fails to revere anything sacred he is profaning the holy premises. Any attack against a sacred cow is therefore profane. On a lower level, actual verbal profanity becomes an effective tactic in defeating the sacred cow. The defenses or reasons for respecting and accepting the revered symbol are so ridiculously irrational that the believers crumble or go into a state of shock before a vulgar question such as, "Do you really believe such crap?" whereas if stated courteously such a question would result in another long ride around the rhetorical ranch. However, the radical must know that with irreverence, as with everything else in life, there is a time and a place. Irreverence simply for irreverence's sake or profanity purely for the sake of profanity becomes the mark of a defensive, fearful, sick, limited individual. If twenty-five years ago I had gone into Chicago's Back of the Yards, practically an all-Catholic community, eating a ham sandwich on a Friday and espousing birth control I would have been rejected as a screwball. If twenty-five years ago I had been quoted in a national news magazine: ". . . The Apostle Paul had the qualities of a true revolutionary leader; without his skill Christ would have been just another statistic—they put about 350 on the cross that year," * I would have been ostracized by organized religion. But now the remarks are quoted with approval in a national magazine. The times and issues have so changed that while such a statement remains irreverent, its acceptance communicates a widespread desire for a new freedom from pieties.

Similarly I would have been denounced twenty-five years ago for stating:

In a mass organization you can't go outside of people's actual experience. I've been asked, for example, why I never talk to a Catholic priest or a Protestant minister or a rabbi in terms of the Judeo-Christian ethic or the Ten Commandments or the Sermon on the Mount. I never talk in those terms. Instead I approach them on the basis of their own self-interest, the welfare of their church, even its physical property.

If I approached them in a moralistic way, it would be outside of their experience, because Christianity and Judeo-Christianity are outside of the experience of organized religion. They would just listen to me and very sympathetically tell me how noble I was. And the moment I walked out they'd call their secretaries in and say, "If that screwball ever shows up again, tell him I'm out." †

Indeed the times have changed and today many now question the rationales which had developed around their sacred concepts. The sacred cows of past theology have been badly shaken by the present generations and, as has frequently been the case in the past, many have privately abandoned their belief in certain sacred cows but timidly have not said so publicly.

Therefore, the radical organizer's irreverence and profanity are purposeful, for he knows that his questions, challenges, or charges are already stewing in the minds of many of his listeners. The radical's pub-

* T. George Harris, "The Battle of the Bible," *Look,* July 27, 1965.

† Marion K. Sanders, "The Professional Radical," *Harper's Magazine,* June, 1965.

lic challenge is irreverent in that he says out loud what others have already silently agreed to. In his irreverence he is not going outside of the experience of his audience, which would be to defeat communication.

Paradoxically the roots of the radical's irreverence toward his present society lie in his reverence for the values and promises of the democratic faith, of the free and open society. He is angry with and hates those parts of the body politic that have broken faith with the future, with the dreams and hopes of a free way of life.

His is a quest for a future: where everyone would have a job, a real job—more than just a paycheck—a job that would be meaningful to society as well as to the worker; a future where everyone would have full opportunities to achieve his potentiality; where education, good housing, health, and full equality for all would be universal; a promised land of peace and plenty; a world where all the revolutionary slogans of the past would come to life: "Love your neighbor as you would love yourself"; "You are your brother's keeper"; "Liberty, Fraternity, Equality"; "All men are created equal"; "Peace and bread"; "For the general welfare"; a world where the Judeo-Christian values and the promise of the American Constitution would be made real.

Each victory will bring a new vision of human happiness, for man's highest end is to create—total fulfillment, total security, would dull the creative drive. Ours is really the quest for uncertainty, for that continuing change which is life. *The pursuit of happiness is never ending—the happiness lies in the pursuit.*

My hopes and dreams when I wrote *Reveille for Radicals* still burn as brightly as before. I have been faithful to my youth.

1968-1969   S.D.A.
Chicago, Illinois

Part I

Call Me Rebel

1

What Is a Radical?

THE PEOPLE of America live everywhere from Back Bay Boston to the Bottoms of Kansas City. From swank Lake Forest, Illinois, to slum Harlem, New York. From the gentlemen farmers of Connecticut to the sharecroppers of Arkansas. From the marble swimming pools of magnificent Bel-Air, California, to the muck of the Flats of Cleveland. From sooty Harlan County, Kentucky, to impeccable Bar Harbor, Maine.

The people of America are red, white, black, yellow, and all the shades in between. Their eyes are blue, black, and brown, and all the shades in between. Their hair is straight, curly, kinky, and most of it in between. They are tall and short, slim and fat, athletic and anaemic, and most of them in between. They are the different peoples of the world becoming more and more the "in between." They are a people creating a new bridge of mankind *in between* the past of narrow nationalistic chauvinism and the horizon of a new mankind—a people of the world. Their face is the face of the future.

The people of America include followers of all the major religions on the face of the earth. They are Christians, regardless of which one of the two hundred or more different major varieties or sects that compose Christianity. They are Baptists, both Northern and Southern, Episcopalians, Lutherans, Catholics, Men-

nonites, Methodists, Mormons, Seventh-Day Adventists, Christian Scientists, and a hundred-odd more.
There are many who believe in Christianity but who
do not have any formal membership in any one
of these organized religious groups. There are Jews,
whether they be Orthodox, Conservative, or Re-
formed. There are Mohammedans, Buddhists, and followers of Confucius. There are atheists and agnostics.
The steeples and the domes of America's houses of
worship are to be found on every hill, in every valley,
and in every nook and cranny of America. From these
houses of worship come the stiff formal Episcopalian
hymns, the wild orgiastic shouts of the Seventh-Day
Adventists or the Holy Rollers, the chants of the syn-
agogue, the liturgical music of the Catholic church, the
singsong medleys of Confucius and Mohammed, and
the cold logic of atheists—all combining into a synthesis of divine faith that is truly the American prayer.

The people of America are the people of the world.
They have come from all corners of the earth. They are
Slavs, Czechs, Germans, Irish, English, Spanish,
French, Russian, Chinese, Japanese, and Afro-Ameri-
cans.

The people of America live as they can. Many of
them are pent up in one-room crumbling shacks and
a few live in penthouses. They live in cold-water flats
and air-conditioned town houses. A vast segment of
our people are confined by color to the dingiest of tenements. In between are many of the *Have-Some-
thing, Want-More's,* in apartments or one-family
homes.

The American people have worked hard. Most of
them have worked with their hands. They hewed their
own log cabins and carved out the railroads, the dams,
and the skyscrapers, that made America what it is.
They have sweated in doing so. They smell like the
people of the world. The *Have's* smell toilet water,
the *Have-Not's* smell just plain toilet.

They speak an American language all their own,

from the "youse guys" of Brooklyn to the "you-alls" of
Georgia. There are New England nasal twangs and the
slow soft drawl of the Far West. Listen to the people of
America talk. Whether you stand on New York's Times
Square, Chicago's State and Madison streets, Kansas
City's Twelfth and Grand, small South St. Paul's Con-
cord Street, Atlanta's Peachtree Street, San Francisco's
Market and Powell, Los Angeles's Hollywood and
Vine, or Butte's Park and Main streets. In New York
they even talk differently from one part of the city to
another, from the soft cultured tones of Park Avenue to
the flat screech of The Bronx.

The people of America behave like the people of the
world. They scratch their itches; in Chicago they belch
in Back of the Yards and they politely burp in the Am-
bassador East. They are sweaty and they are suave.
Their interests range far out over society or they are
narrowly confined to their street. They are grubby and
grand. They look and dress differently. From the blue
denim Levis of the West to the black full-dress suit of
the East. From the patched gingham dress of the
sharecropper's wife to the latest French importation
on Philadelphia's Main Line.

What do Americans eat? They eat mulligan stew
alongside the railroad tracks or they eat breast of
guinea hen in the dining cars that ride over the tracks.
They eat smörgåsbord and they eat hot dogs. They eat
pig's knuckles and they eat gefüllte fish. They eat
chicken booya and they eat corned beef and cabbage.
They eat hominy and grits and Italian spaghetti. They
eat hot cakes and syrup and crêpes suzettes. They eat
apple pie and they eat strudel. They eat ham and eggs
and they eat octopus. They eat steak and they eat Russian borscht. They eat corn on the cob and Wiener-
schnitzel. They drink Coca-Cola and Heineken's beer.

They have fried chicken and hot biscuits at their
church socials and chicken Kiev at sophisticated night
spots. They eat baked beans at the Automat and
French food in the Bull and Bear restaurant at the

Waldorf. They are vegetarians, food faddists, and vita-
min takers. They eat what their forefathers ate and
their forefathers came from everywhere. The diet of
America is the diet of the world.

The American people were, in the beginning, Revolutionaries and Tories. The American people ever
since have been Revolutionaries and Tories. They have
been Revolutionaries and Tories regardless of the labels of the past and present. Regardless of whether
they were Federalists, Democrat-Republicans, Whigs,
Know-Nothings, Free Soilers, Unionists or Confeder-
ates, Populists, Republicans, Democrats, Socialists,
Communists, or Progressives. They have been and are
profiteers and patriots. They have been and are conservatives, liberals, and radicals.

The clash of Radicals, conservatives, and liberals
which makes up America's political history opens the
door to the most fundamental question of what is
America? How do the people of America feel? It is in
this feeling that the real story of America is written.
There were and are a number of Americans—few, to
be sure—filled with deep feeling for people. They
know that people are the stuff that makes up the
dream of democracy. These few were and are the
American radicals and the only way that we can understand the American radical is to understand what
we mean by this feeling for and with people. Psychiatrists, psychologists, sociologists, and other learned
students call this feeling "identification" and have
elaborate and complicated explanations about what
it means. For our purposes it boils down to the simple
question, How do you feel about people?

Do you like people? Most people claim that they
like people with, of course, a "few exceptions." When
the exceptions are added together it becomes clear
that they include a vast majority of the people. It becomes equally clear that most people like just a few
people, their kind of people, and either do not actively

care for or actively dislike most of the "other" people.

You are white, native-born, and Protestant. Do you like people? You like your family, your friends, some of your business associates (not too many of them), and some of your neighbors. Do you like Catholics, Irish, Italians, Jews, Poles, Mexicans, Negroes, Puerto Ricans, and Chinese? Do you regard them with the warm feeling of fellow human beings or with a cold contempt symbolized in Papists, Micks, Wops, Kikes, Hunkies, Greasers, Niggers, Spics, and Chinks? If you are one of those people who think of people in these derogatory terms, then you don't like people.

You may object to this and say that you do not fall into this classification. You don't call people by such names. You are broad-minded and respect other peoples if they *know their place*—and that place is not close to your own affections. You feel that you are really very tolerant. The chances are that you are an excellent representative of the great American class of Mr. But. Haven't you met Mr. But? Sure, you have. You have met him downtown at civic luncheons. You have met him at Community Fund meetings, at housing conferences, at political rallies, and most likely he has greeted you every morning from the mirror in your bathroom. Mr. But is the man who is broad-minded, sensible practical, and proud of his Christianity. You have heard him talk many times, just as you have heard yourself talk many times. What does he say? Listen to the great American, Mr. But:

"Now nobody can say that I'm not a friend of the Mexicans or that I am prejudiced, BUT——"

"Nobody can say that I'm anti-Semitic. Why, some of my best friends are Jews, BUT——"

"Surely nobody can think of me as a reactionary, BUT——"

"I don't think anyone in this room feels more sympathetic toward the Negroes than I do. I've always had a number of them working for me, BUT——"

"It's perfectly all right for these people to have equal opportunities for work, and after all we are all Americans, aren't we? BUT——"

"Anybody knows that I would be the first to fight against this injustice, BUT——"

"Labor unions are all right, BUT——"

"Sure, I say that all Americans should have the right to live any place they want to regardless of race, color, or creed, BUT——"

You are very probably a typical MR. BUT. You make "tolerant" jokes behind the backs of your fellow Americans, about their clothes, complexions, speech, manners, and names. You regard yourself as tolerant, and in that one adjective you most fittingly describe yourself. You really don't *like* people you *tolerate* them. You are very tolerant, MR. BUT. You leave a luncheon meeting at which you sat next to a Negro and talked with him (and you tell your friends about it for months to come). You are so flushed and filled with your own goodness that if the thought could father the deed you would take flight on your new angelic wings.

Thomas Jefferson saw this very clearly in his letter to Henry Lee on August 10, 1824:

Men by their constitution are naturally divided into two parties: 1. Those who fear and distrust the people, and wish to draw all powers from them into the hands of the higher classes.

2. Those who identify themselves with the people, have confidence in them, cherish and consider them as the most honest and safe, although not the most wise depository of the public interests. In every country these two parties exist, and in every one where they are free to think, speak, and write, they will declare themselves. Call them, therefore, Liberals and Serviles, Jacobins and Ultras, Whigs and Tories, Republicans and Federalists, Aristocrats and Democrats, or by whatever name you please, they are the same parties still and pursue the same object. The last appellation of Aristocrats and Democrats is the true one expressing the essence of all.

During Jefferson's lifetime the words democrat and radical were synonymous. Just as people then were divided between those who feared and disliked people and those who liked them, so is Jefferson's observation as true today as it was in 1824 and as true as it always has been since the beginning of mankind.

There were those few, and there will be more, who really liked people, loved people—all people. They were the human torches setting aflame the hearts of men so that they passionately fought for the rights of their fellow men, all men. They were hated, feared, and branded as *radicals*. They wore the epithet of *radical* as a badge of honor. They fought for the right of men to govern themselves, for the right of men to walk erect as free men and not grovel before kings, for the Bill of Rights, for the abolition of slavery, for public education, and for everything decent and worth while. They loved men and fought for them. Their neighbor's misery was their misery. They acted as they believed.

So you are an Irish Catholic? The one who suffers from the white, native-born Protestant, Mr. But. You are the one who accuses him of prejudice! Let's take a good look at you. Do you like people? Of course you do. But what about Protestants? What about Jews? What about Negroes and Chinese? What about your fellow Catholics—Italians, Poles, Lithuanians, Slovaks, Mexicans, Puerto Ricans, and others? What about your fellow Irish? How many of you look down on them as inferior to yourselves? Don't you call your own illiterate and poor "Shanty Irish"? How many of your own frustrations have you rationalized by blaming it on "Catholic" prejudice? Is the Catholic Church so very important in your life because it represents a spiritual sanctuary or because it's a political power for jobs and material success? There are a few of you that have gone out to battle against narrow nationalism, anti-Semitism, Jim Crow, and for the bettering of the economic conditions of all mankind. Those few did this because they were devoted to the welfare of all of their

fellow men. To them Catholicism was a living everyday faith and way of life. They were real Catholics
in spite of the disapproval of parts of the formal
church. There were your radicals. They are your proud
heritage.

So you're a Jew. Maybe you're one of the few living
on Park Avenue, or in the upper sixties. You bitterly resent anti-Semitism and regard prejudiced people as
uncivilized, irreligious, and definitely un-American.
Let's take a look at you. How do you feel about the
frock-coated Jews in the Williamsburg section of
Brooklyn? You don't like them. You think of them
as loud, uncouth, and dirty. You don't like the way
they smile or the way they talk. You say it is bad for
the Jews. Maybe you are a Spanish Jew and you look
down on the German Jew, or you are a German Jew
and you look down with utter contempt upon the Russian and Polish Jew. Maybe you're so intent on social
prestige, becoming accepted in the best clubs, living
in the more exclusive residential sections, fraternizing
with the so-called best people, that you reject all
Jews. On the other hand, many of you may be fighting
valiantly the prejudice in parts of the American system
that is centered against you and your fellow Jews.
While you are fighting are you thinking of the same
un-American hatred that is aimed at Negroes, Mexicans, Puerto Ricans, and all other minorities? If you
think only of yourself, then in the last analysis you too
are a Mr. and Mrs. But. There are very few of you,
just as there are very few of the Protestants and
Catholics, who really like people—the few who fought
on the picket line, through the printed page, before
the crumbling walls of Madrid, and in the South
against the lynch mobs and for the sharecroppers.
They fight for all. They, as radicals, resent injustice to
any man. Many Jews have pointed out that the radicals from their group are few and far between. That
is true. It's as true as it is for any other group. For,

after all, the people who really like their fellow men
are few and far between.

So you're a Negro. You're a Negro and you deeply
resent the hypocrisy and the bigotry of the whites. You
hate Jim Crow with all your heart. You live in a prison
of prejudice. Your home is in the worst section of the
city. You don't have an equal chance for a job. You go
to college and when you graduate you're given a job
as a doorman. You're barred from the best jobs and the
house next door, and you live in just plain unadulter-
ated hell. Your life is still what one little Negro school-
girl wrote when asked by the teacher to write an es-
say on punishment for Hitler: "Dress him up in a
black skin and make him live in the United States."
You have white friends who pride themselves on not
being prejudiced. They meet with you at various civic
affairs, pat you on the back, and underneath it all still
hold you off at arm's length and regard you as a
Negro. They talk in terms of patience and say that
there will come a time in the mystical future when we
will all sit together and eat pie in the sky. It's the difference between Northern Jim Crow and his Southern
brother. One may be more subtle but every bit as cruel.
They're both part of the same iniquitous family. You
resent all that, but how do you reconcile fighting
against prejudice and being prejudiced? You are predominantly Protestants. How do you feel about Jews?
How do you feel about Catholics? How do you feel
about your own people? You have a gradation of
color where light-skinned people feel superior to dark-
skinned. You refer to one another in anger with the
same hateful adjectives you resent when they are
used by whites. Many of your so-called leaders are
servile to white interests. When some of your own have
fought for decency, dignity, equality, and every principle embodied in the Revolutionary rights of America, some of you have stamped him a *radical*. Because
that fighter incurs the displeasure of the ruling whites,

some of you have become apprehensive of white retribution and so you have turned on him with terrible bitterness and refused to follow. You don't like people any more than do those who don't like you. You too have your share of MR. BUT's.

So you're a Pole. You hate being called a Hunkie. You resent being assigned menial jobs—common labor. You resent being looked down upon as slow-witted—good only for manual work and living across the tracks. You denounce these prejudices as un-American and undemocratic. How do you feel about people? Well, we'll have a look at you. You're clannish in your Catholicism to the extent that you want your own special churches. You resent the Irish domination in churches and politics and hate the Irish for it. How do you feel about Jews? Many of you hate them with an unparalleled bitterness. That hatred is illustrated in many little sayings. You have a proverb that when a Pole has no money he comes to church and when he does have money he goes to the Jews. You say it with the same feeling that you say he goes to the devil. Many of you hate Negroes too, just as deeply. You too have had your great radicals, those few who really liked all people. Those who fought the battles of others—only they never thought in terms of "others"; they couldn't because they were real radicals.

So you're a Mexican. You are segregated and subjected to many of the indignities of the Negro. You are set apart and looked down upon. You resent this. But how do you feel about people? Many of your Mexican leaders in Southern California resisted the efforts of the Negroes to unite in a common bond against segregation. They said that the Negroes were trying to pull them down to their level. They take pleasure in referring to themselves as Spanish-Americans, and bitterly resent the feeling on the part of North Americans that Mexicans are not "white." From one corner of their mouths they protest segregation and discrimination and argue forthrightly for justice and equality, and

from the other corner they condemn the Negro as an
inferior race. Those Mexicans who tried to organize
against the destructive American forces that are responsible for inequality of opportunity, economic insecurity, and lack of educational opportunities have
been hated as radicals and many of the respectable
Mexican leaders, including the religious leaders, have
denounced them as radicals. These radicals have
fought for union with all other minority groups; as a
matter of fact, with all peoples. They have fought because they like people, all people.

Where are America's radicals? They were with Pat-
rick Henry in the Virginia Hall of Burgesses; they
were with Sam Adams in Boston; they were with that
peer of all American radicals, Tom Paine, from the
distribution of *Common Sense* through those dark
days of the American Revolution—"the times that try
men's souls; the summer soldier and the sunshine pa-
triot will, in this crisis, shrink from the service of his
country; but he that stands it NOW, deserves the love
and thanks of man and woman." They were again
with Tom Paine when he fought to abolish slavery in
the Declaration of Independence; they were high on
the list of public enemies of the American Tories who
fumed at the three Toms, "Tom Jefferson, Tom Paine,
and Tom Devil."

The American radicals were in the colonies grimly
forcing the addition of the Bill of Rights to our Constitution. They stood at the side of Tom Jefferson in
the first big battle between the Tories of Hamilton
and the American people. They founded and fought
in the Loco-Focos. They were in the first union strike
in America and they fought for the distribution of the
western lands to the masses of people instead of the
few. They were everywhere, fighting and dying to free
their fellow Americans regardless of their race or
creed. They were in the shadows of the Underground

Railroad, and they openly rode in the bright sunlight with John Brown to Harpers Ferry. They were in the halls of Congress with Thaddeus Stevens, bitterly and uncompromisingly fighting for the complete economic and political freedom of their Negro fellow Americans. They were with Horace Mann fighting for the extension of educational opportunities. They carried the torch for the first public schools. They were in the vanguard of the Populist Party leading the Western rebellion against Eastern conservatism. They built the American Labor movement from the Knights of Labor through the American Federation of Labor, the I.W.W., and finally spearheaded the fateful drive that culminated in the Congress of Industrial Organizations. They were with Wendell Phillips fighting for labor's right of equality of opportunity. They were with Peter Cooper fighting the ruthlessness of industrial barons. They hovered around Walt Whitman, who, seeing American democracy being betrayed, wrote *Democratic Vistas*. They were with Henry George attacking monopoly in *Progress and Poverty*. They were with Edward Bellamy, who saw an America where the common good was being subordinated to private selfishness and wrote *Looking Backward*. They were with John P. Altgeld, the great governor of Illinois who refused to use state power against labor unions, who defied public opinion and pardoned the anarchists unjustly convicted of the Haymarket bombing. They were with those great muckrakers Henry D. Lloyd, Lincoln Steffens, and Upton Sinclair in their relentless exposures of brutal oppressions, injustice, and corruption.

Many of their deeds are not and never will be recorded in America's history. They were among the grimy men in the dust bowl, they sweated with the sharecroppers, they were at the side of the Okies facing the California vigilantes, they stood before the fury of lynch mobs, they were on the picket lines gazing unflinchingly at the threatening, flushed, angry faces

of the police. They were with Chicago's Catholic
Bishop Sheil when, ignoring threats from the highest
vested authorities, he took his place at the side of thousands of packinghouse workers who had squared off
against the hitherto invulnerable meat trust.

America's radicals are to be found wherever and
whenever America moves close to the fulfillment of
its democratic dream. Whenever America's hearts
are breaking, there American radicals were and are.
America was begun by its radicals. America was built
by its radicals. The hope and future of America lies
with its radicals.

What is the American radical? The radical is that
unique person who actually believes what he says. He
is that person to whom the common good is the greatest personal value. He is that person who genuinely
and completely believes in mankind. The radical is
so completely identified with mankind that he personally shares the pain, the injustices, and the suffer-
ings of all his fellow men.

For the radical the bell tolls unceasingly and every
man's struggle is his fight.

The radical is not fooled by shibboleths and fa-
çades. He faces issues squarely and does not hide his
cowardice behind the convenient cloak of rationalization. The radical refuses to be diverted by superficial
problems. He is completely concerned with fundamental causes rather than current manifestations. He
concentrates his attack on the heart of the issue.

What does the radical want? He wants a world in
which the worth of the individual is recognized. He
wants the creation of a kind of society where all of
man's potentialities could be realized; a world where
man could live in dignity, security, happiness, and
peace—a world based on a morality of mankind.

To these ends radicals struggle to eradicate all
those evils which anchor mankind in the mire of war,
fears, misery, and demoralization. The radical is
concerned not only with the economic welfare of the

bodies of mankind but also with the freedom of the
minds of man. It is for this that he attacks all those
parts of any system that tend to make man a robot.
It is for this that he opposes all circumstances which
destroy the souls of men and make them fearful,
petty, worried, dull sheep in men's clothing. The radical is dedicated to the destruction of the roots of all
fears, frustrations, and insecurity of man, whether
they be material or spiritual. The radical wants to
see man truly free. Not just free economically and
politically but also free socially. When the radical
says complete freedom he means just that.

The radical believes that all peoples should have a
high standard of food, housing, and health. The radical is impatient with talk of the "closing of frontiers"
or the "end of the frontiers." He thinks only in terms
of human frontiers, which are as limitless as the horizons. The radical believes intensely in the possibilities
of man and hopes fervently for the future.

The radical places human rights far above property
rights. He is for universal, free public education and
recognizes this as fundamental to the democratic way
of life. He will be for local control but will condemn
local abuse of public education—whether it be discrimination or corruption—that denies equal education to anyone, and will insist if necessary upon its
correction by national laws and the use of governmental authority to enforce those laws—but at the
same time he will bitterly oppose complete federal
control of education. He will fight for individual
rights and against centralized power. He will usually
be found battling in defense of local rights against
federal usurpations of power, but he knows that ever
since the Tories attacked the Continental Congress as
an invasion of local rights, "local rights"—or, as the
term has come to be known, "States' rights"—have
been the star-spangled Trojan horse of Tory reaction.
It is for this reason that the American radical fre-

quently shifts his position on this issue, in keeping with his fundamental beliefs in the rights of man.

The radical is deeply interested in social planning but just as deeply suspicious of, and antagonistic to, any idea of plans that work from the top down. Democracy to him is working from the bottom up.

The radical is a staunch defender of minority rights but will combat any minority which tries to use the club of minority rights to bludgeon into unconsciousness the will of the majority.

In short, the American radical, by his individual actions, may appear to be the epitome of inconsistency, but when judged on the basis of his ideals, philosophy, and objectives, he is a living definition of consistency.

The radical believes completely in *real* equality of opportunity for all peoples regardless of race, color, or creed. He insists on full employment for economic security but is just as insistent that man's work should not only provide economic security but also be such as to satisfy the creative desires within all men. The radical feels that the importance of a job is not only in its individual economic return but also in its general social significance. The radical knows that man is not just an economic man. The complete man is one who is making a definite contribution to the general social welfare and who is a vital part of that community of interests, values, and purposes that makes life and people meaningful. The complete man needs a complete job—a job for the heart as well as the hand—a job where he can say to himself, "What I do is important and has its place."

The American radical will fight privilege and power, whether it be inherited or acquired by any small group, whether it be political or financial or organized creed. He curses a caste system, aware that it exists despite all patriotic denials. He will fight conservatives, whether they are business or labor lead-

ers. He will fight any concentration of power hostile
to a broad, popular democracy, whether he finds it in
financial circles or in politics.

The radical recognizes that constant dissension and
conflict is and has been the fire under the boiler of
democracy. He firmly believes in that brave saying of
a brave people, "Better to die on your feet than to live
on your knees!" The radical may resort to the sword
but when he does he is not filled with hatred against
those individuals whom he attacks. He hates these individuals not as persons but as symbols representing
ideas or interests which he believes to be inimical to
the welfare of the people. This is the reason why radicals, although frequently they have embarked upon
revolutions, have rarely resorted to personal terrorism.

To the general public radicals may appear to be
persons of violence. But if radicals are stormy and
fighting on the outside, they possess an inner dignity.
It is the dignity that can come only from consistency
of conscience and conduct. The first part of the Prayer
of St. Francis of Assisi expresses to a large extent the
radical's hopes, aspirations, dreams, and philosophy:

*Lord, make me an instrument of Thy peace; where there is
hatred, let me sow love; where there is doubt, faith; where
there is despair, hope; where there is darkness, light; and
where there is sadness, joy.*

But let no man or combination of men who ruth-
lessly exploit their fellow men assume because of the
nobility and spiritual quality of the radical's hopes
that he will not stand up for the fulfillment of this
prayer, for next to this prayer he carries within him
the words of Jehovah:

*When I whet my glittering sword, and my hand taketh hold
on Judgment: I will render vengeance unto my enemies,
and those that hate me will I requite.*
*I will make my arrows drunken with blood, and my
sword shall devour flesh; from the blood of the slain and
of the captives, from the crushed head of the enemy.*

There are many liberals who claim the same objectives in life that characterize the philosophy of the radical, but there are as many clear lines of distinction between radicals and liberals as there are between liberals and conservatives. There is a tremendous significance to that common saying that a man is a radical at twenty-one, a liberal at thirty-one, and a conservative at forty. The young man of twenty-one still has certain burning ideals. He still has faith in life and hope in progress. He is still naïve enough to take what he says literally. He is still young enough not to have acquired a vested material interest and the attendant suspicions of any social change which might jeopardize it. He still hasn't reached the point of believing that "all men are created equal" is nice in theory but taboo in practice. He has not become civilized to the point of assimilating all the prejudices and hate which permeate so large a portion of our lives. He still has some of the simplicity and decency of the child. He still likes, and actually expects to be liked in return. He still is not filled with the virus of driving personal ambition, with sophistication and its accompanying constellation of rationalizations, and with a cynicism which is a cover-up for the deep fear of the future. He is a brave young man whose life is not cluttered up with prejudices and fears. He is a radical. Radicals always remain young in spite of the passage of years. That is one of the differences between the radical and the liberal. There are others.

Liberals like people with their heads, radicals like people with both their heads and their *hearts*. Liberals talk passionately of the rights of minority groups; protest against the denial of political and voting rights, against segregation, against anti-Semitism, and against all other inhuman practices of humanity. However, when these same liberals emerge from their meetings, rallies, and passage of resolutions and find themselves seated next to a Negro in a public conveyance they tend to shrink back slightly. They belong to professional organizations and social clubs whose membership is exclusive—*exclusive* of Jews, Negroes, and many other minorities. They tell you that they disapprove of the practice, but nevertheless continue their membership. Intellectually they subscribe to all of the principles of the American Revolution and the Constitution of the United States, but in their hearts they do not. They are a strange breed of hybrids who have radical minds and conservative hearts. They really like people *only* with their heads. The radical genuinely likes people.

Liberals regard themselves as well informed and well balanced. They refer to radicals as "cranks." They forget, however, that the definition of a crank is an object that makes revolutions.

Liberals, in common with many conservatives, lay claim to the precious quality of impartiality, of cold objectivity, and to a sense of mystical impartial justice which enables them to view both sides of an issue. Since there are always at least two sides to every question and all justice on one side involves a certain degree of injustice to the other side, liberals are hesitant to act. Their opinions are studded with "but on the other hand." Caught on the horns of this dilemma they are paralyzed into immobility. They become utterly incapable of action. They discuss and discuss and end in disgust.

Liberals charge radicals with passionate partisanship. To this accusation the radical's jaw tightens as he snaps, "Guilty! We are partisan for the people. Furthermore, we know that all people are partisan. The only nonpartisan people are those who are dead. You too are partisan—if not for the people, then for whom?"

Liberals utter bold words at meetings; they strut, grimace belligerently, and then issue a weasel-worded statement "which has tremendous implications, if read between the lines." They endlessly pass resolutions and endlessly do nothing. They sit calmly, dispassionately, studying the issue; judging both sides; they sit and sit still. The radical does not sit frozen by cold objectivity. He sees injustice and strikes at it with hot passion. He is a man of decision and action. There is a saying that the difference between a liberal and a radical is that the liberal is one who walks out of the room when the argument turns into a fight.

Liberals have distorted egotistical concepts of their self-importance in the general social scheme. They deliberate as ponderously and as lengthily as though their decisions would cause the world to shake and tremble. Theirs is truly a perfect case of the mountain laboring and bringing forth a mouse—a small, white, pink-eyed mouse. The fact is that outside of their own intimate associates few know of or give a hang what these liberal groups decide. They truly fit the old description that "A liberal is one who puts his foot down firmly on thin air."

The support given by liberals to some radical measures is to be understood in the explanation a wealthy French farmer gave when he voted for Socialism. "I vote for Socialism always and steadily," he said, "because there isn't going to be any Socialism."

A complacent society tolerantly views the turbulent atmospheric noise of liberal minds with the old childhood slogan of "Sticks and stones may break my bones, but names will never hurt me." Let the liberal turn to the course of action, the course of all radicals, and the amused look vanishes from the face of society as it snarls, "That's radical!" Society has good reason to fear the radical. Every shaking advance of mankind toward equality and justice has come from the radical. He hits, he hurts, he is dangerous. Conservative interests know that while liberals are most adept at breaking their own necks with their tongues, radicals are most adept at breaking the necks of conservatives.

A fundamental difference between liberals and radicals is to be found in the issue of power. Liberals fear power or its application. They labor in confusion over the significance of power and fail to recognize that only through the achievement and constructive use of power can people better themselves. They talk glibly of people lifting themselves by their own bootstraps but fail to realize that nothing can be lifted or moved except through power. This fear of popular use of power is reflected in what has become the motto of liberals, "We agree with your objectives but not with your tactics." This has been the case throughout the history of America. Through every great crisis, including the American Revolution, there were thousands of well-meaning liberals who always cried out, "We agree with you that America should be free, but we disagree that it is necessary to have a bloody revolution." "We agree that slavery should be eliminated but we disagree with the turmoil of civil war." Every issue involving power and its use has always carried in its wake the liberal backwash of agreeing with the objective but disagreeing with the tactics.

Radicals precipitate the social crisis by action—by using power. Liberals may then timidly follow along or else, as in most cases, be swept forward along the course set by radicals, but all because of forces unloosed by radical action. They are forced to positive action only in spite of their desires.

There are other differences between liberals and radicals. Liberals protest; radicals rebel. Liberals become indignant; radicals become fighting mad and go into action. Liberals do not modify their personal lives and what they give to a cause is a small part of their lives; radicals give themselves to the cause. Liberals give and take oral arguments; radicals give and take the hard, dirty, bitter way of life. Liberals frequently achieve high places of respectability, ranging from the Supreme Court to Congress; the names of radicals are rarely enscribed in marble but burn eternally in the hearts of man. Liberals have tender beliefs and are filled with repugnance at the grime, the sordidness, the pain, the persecution, and the heart-break of battle; radicals have tough convictions which are calloused by the rough road of direct action. Liberals play the game of life with white and occasionally red chips; with the radical it's only blue chips, and all the chips are always down. Liberals dream dreams; radicals build the world of men's dreams.

These are the marks and ideals of the perfect radical. Perfection is scarcely realized in mankind, but it is a guidepost to the ultimate. We should never forget that just as it would be almost impossible to find any man a full and perfect Christian or Jew, so it is impossible to find that radical whose life and character fully measure up to these characteristics. People are not all good or all bad, neither angels nor devils. In the actual history of mankind we find few whose thoughts and actions place them even to a microscopic degree beyond the midpoint of the spectrum. There are those who have lived nearly all of their mortal lives at the lower end, but for a fleeting moment, for a month or for some years, have seen the blinding vision at the other end of the spectrum and risked all in an action or a deed that was unmistakably radical. These men and women are for our purposes radicals.

Only a perfectionist would define a radical as one who has been consistently radical throughout his lifetime. To look for the radical who is radical on all issues is also to search for consummate purity. The criterion as to what is a radical can be used only in a relative sense; not only to see if a significant part of a person's life was given to a human service, not only to evaluate the importance of the contribution to mankind, but to evaluate the radical's importance to the making of that contribution.

2

Where Is the Radical Today?

DEEP in the cradle of organized labor America's radicals restlessly toss in their sleep—but they sleep. There they continue to dream of labor and the world of the future. The belief that labor and progress should be one and indivisible is, however, not a point of view monopolized by American radicals.

Throughout Western civilization, radicals tied their destiny to the organized labor movement. To them the labor movement was the key to the door of the future world of economic justice and the social betterment of mankind. The labor movement has been as much of an ideological foundation to all left-wing thinkers as the Ten Commandments and the Golden Rule are to devout religionists.

The burning conviction that organized labor is the only hope for the future has been traditionally so deeply rooted in the minds of radicals that in some parts of the world it is tantamount to heresy even to raise the issue of whether organized labor as we know it ever did, does today, or ever will present the road to the good life. In any appraisal of institutions and movements there is a constant danger that our own complete acceptance and passionate devotion to a cause may preclude any critical scrutiny of that very cause. It is that strange paradox that the things we primarily take for granted are the last to be questioned. Too often, this has been true with reference to any evaluation of the labor movement on the part of radicals. It is time that we look into the character of the labor movement in order to ascertain to what extent, if any, the purposes and philosophy of labor are consonant with that of the radical.

The simplest approach to this problem would be a comparison of the future desired by radicals as over against that future desired by the organized labor movement. First, what do radicals want of the future? From a general point of view, liberals and radicals desire progress. In this they differ from conservatives, for while a conservative wishes to conserve the status quo, liberals ask for change and radicals fight for change. They desire a world rid of those destructive forces from which issue wars. They want to do away with economic injustice, insecurity, unequal opportunities, prejudice, bigotry, imperialism, all chauvinistic barriers of isolationism and other nationalistic neuroses. They want a world where life for man will be guided by a morality that is meaningful—and where the values of good and evil will be measured not in terms of money morals but social morals. For these and many other reasons they face the challenge of the future with anticipation and hope.

Radicals want to advance from the jungle of laissez-faire capitalism to a world worthy of the name of human civilization. They hope for a future where the means of economic production will be owned by all of the people instead of just a comparative handful. They feel that this minority control of production facilities is injurious to the large masses of people not only because of economic monopolies but because the political power inherent in this form of centralized economy does not augur well for an ever expanding democratic way of life. Radicals want to see the established political rights or political freedom of the common man augmented by economic freedom. They believe that Lincoln's statement that a nation cannot exist half-free and half-slave is applicable to the entire world and includes economic as well as political freedom. In short, radicals are convinced that the marriage of political rights to economic rights will produce a social morality in which the Golden Rule will replace the gold standard.

Possessed of this sketch of a world to be, radicals find themselves adrift in the stormy sea of capitalism. In this sea there are two main currents—one called organized industry and the other organized labor. Radicals have been convinced that the current of organized industry leads direct to perdition, and they have little doubt but that the current of organized labor flows to the promised land. If the facts should indicate that both of these currents are actually running in the same direction, then our radicals may find their faith in labor in danger of foundering. Has the faith of the radicals been justified?

Parallel with the centralized organization of business, labor, too, has developed a centralized organization. This organized labor movement, which includes tremendous organized economic power, is also being directed toward the securing of political power for its own ends. The question that presents itself is what, if any, differences are there between the ultimate objectives of organized industry and those of organized labor?

Suppose we pierce through the flaming slogans, militant statements, noble writings, and dramatic stories and look into the workings, the purposes, and the philosophy of the organized labor movement in terms of its contrast to the character of organized capital.

In recent times it has become increasingly clear that

the organized labor movement *as it is constituted to-day* is as much a concomitant of a capitalist economy as is capital. Organized labor is predicated upon the basic premise of collective bargaining between employers and employees. This premise can obtain only in an employer-employee type of society. If the labor movement is to maintain its own identity and security, it must of necessity protect that kind of society. This fact has been tacitly recognized by both leaders of industry and leaders of labor. Eric Johnston, once president of the United States Chamber of Commerce and certainly in his own right a representative of industry, stressed this very point in an article called "Your Stake in Capitalism":

A CIO leader in Washington had good sense when he remarked the other day: "I would rather bargain with any private employer than with any bureaucrat. The bureaucrat has jails." [1]

The self-interest of organized businesses solely in profits and in the securing of their own identity and perpetuation of their own existence has likewise expressed itself within the organized labor movement. As labor unions have become strong, wealthy, fat, and respectable, they have behaved more and more like organized business. In many cases their courses have run so parallel that in a basic sense organized labor has become a partner of organized business. The illustrations of this fact are legion, and are found in practically all of the great variety of labor unions.

A critical contrast of the political philosophy and operations of organized labor and organized capital reveals the same difference as exists between their economic programs—one of structure rather than substance. The political policy of organized labor runs parallel to its economic policy—a foursquare stand for a system of monopolistic capitalist economy. While labor proposes certain modifications, once again

[1] *The Reader's Digest* (February 1943), p. 1.

it should be emphasized that these are modifications in form rather than in content. The organized labor movement has with rare exception always opposed revolutionary action aimed at the destruction of monopoly capitalism. The hatred and opposition of big business toward all foes of the status quo is fully shared and participated in by the leaders of the labor movements. They must be opposed to socialism, communism or any other philosophy which would destroy private ownership of industry or private employment. From their point of view, the introduction of a socialistic society would mean the death knell of the present organized labor movement. If the working classes were to assume political control of the economy and society, there would be little point in the continuation of the present type of labor unions. As has been said earlier, the function of a labor union is first of all to bargain collectively between employers and employees.

Those who claim that labor possesses a fundamentally different program from monopoly capital always point out that after all the organized labor movement in America is young and it has not even achieved political power and has never had a chance to demonstrate what it would do if it secured power. However, there are many who are impatient with this perennial "youth" of the organized labor movement in America. It was born in Philadelphia in 1827, which makes it just about as old as the labor union movement of Great Britain.

In the American political scene, the practices of American labor movements have not differed from those of big business. Labor has, just as big business has, dealt politically wherever and with whomever it could with one main objective—to secure benefits for itself. The character and the general philosophy of the political leader has meant nothing, so long as he was "good" to labor. The point is that labor will deal where it can.

During the early days when a union is being organized in the face of almost unanimous opposition it has to fight every inch of the way. It sees issues clearly and forges a set of ideals out of the fire of battle. It will bitterly condemn the corruption of the police, the partisanship and distortion of the press, and the viciousness of the entire system. But as this same union grows, as it begins to acquire a vested interest in the system, as it begins to be accepted and accorded a place, it sheds its revolutionary idealism as quickly as the average revolutionary soapbox orator changes when he gets a few thousand dollars in his pocket. He does not want any change of a system which will take away *his* thousands.

The history of all established labor unions is incontrovertible evidence of the same evolution. Those unions that are well established, respectable, and plump with power and prosperity express the kind of philosophy and political participation which damns them in the eyes of both radicals and liberals as citadels of conservative reaction. A look at the history of these unions will show that in the early days of their organization they were staunch champions of liberty, equality, justice, and all other principles cherished by radicals and liberals. They fought for bread, but as they came into their own in the monopolistic capitalist economy, they too sat down and ate cake.

In the field of race relations the record of organized labor is sickeningly similar to that of organized business. Racial bigotry is practiced by such a large number of unions that it would be difficult to say that they are more emancipated from prejudice than the general population. In the 1943 American Federation of Labor Convention[2] A. Phillip Randolph, the prominent Negro labor leader, charged that the Interna-

[2] *Report of the Proceedings of the Sixty-third Annual Convention of the American Federation of Labor.* Held at Boston, Mass., October 4–14, 1943.

tional Association of Machinists, affiliated with the
American Federation of Labor, actually excluded
Negroes by provision in its ritual. He went on to list
other unions which bar Negroes in their constitu-
tions:

American Federation of Labor affiliates—Airline
Pilots Association; Commercial Telegraphers Union;
National Organization of Masters, Mates and Pilots;
Order of Railroad Telegraphers; Railway Mail Associa-
tion; Switchmen's Union of North America; American
Wire Weavers' Protective Association.

Unaffiliated organizations—Brotherhood of Locomotive Engineers; Brotherhood of Locomotive Firemen and Enginemen; Brotherhood of Railroad Train-
men; Railroad Yardmasters of America; Railroad
Yardmasters of North America; Order of Railway Con-
ductors; American Train Dispatchers' Association.

There are unions that have no formal constitutional
or ritual restrictions against Negroes, but nevertheless
bar them by tacit consent.

Then there have been those unions that openly
practice segregation, admitting Negroes only to special *auxiliary* memberships. This kind of segregated
or *auxiliary* union has been Jim Crow in its most
primitive form—openly proclaiming a racial status
within the union whereby the *auxiliary* is to the union
as a peon or serf is to a feudal noble. Even the colonies of the British Empire had more to say about
their destiny than these *auxiliary* unions. They have
not been permitted to participate or even attend national union conventions, they have been denied any
vote or opportunity in the appointment or election of
their representatives, they have had nothing whatever
to say about the administration of the international
union, they have been permitted only to pay their
dues and assessments. This is even worse than just a
problem of race relations. It is a direct attack against
the very soul of America, against the rallying cry of

the American Revolution, "Taxation without representation."

When the Fair Employment Practices Committee investigated discrimination against the Negroes in the Pacific Coast industries during World War II, big business pointed the finger of responsibility at organized labor. The companies emphasized that provisions of a master agreement between the union and themselves provided a union closed shop and that the latter was wholly responsible for the failure to hire qualified Negro workers. It was pointed out that a number of skilled Negro workers were unable to work in the shipyard because their personal pride and dignity would not permit the acceptance of serf status in the Boilermakers Union *auxiliary*.

There are many other common varieties of racial discrimination in the organized labor unions. Only a decision of the United States Supreme Court prevented the Brotherhood of Locomotive Firemen and Enginemen from closing all employment opportunities to Negro workers except in jobs of the most menial type in the Louisville and Nashville Railroad Company. Under the Railroad Labor Act this particular railroad union had been granted the power of exclusive bargaining representation. Since Negro workers were barred from union membership and since union membership was required for the job, it meant that Negroes were not only ineligible for those jobs but even that Negroes working at common labor were denied any representation in collective bargaining.

It became an annual tradition of the American Federation of Labor conventions for A. Phillip Randolph to denounce the un-American, fascistic racial discrimination practiced in so many American Federation of Labor unions. Its main effect was to cause a general exodus of labor leaders from the convention hall, whence they streamed into adjacent pubs to drink whisky and curse until they got the word that "the Nigger has finished shooting off his mouth and it's okay to come back again."

Brave attacks against the lack of democracy in the organized labor movement are customarily countered with pious resolutions which are written in words of brotherly love but come from hearts full of the bitterness of gall and wormwood. Many important labor officials conspicuously and publicly wave the torch of human rights and racial equality with their right hand while their left hand is busily engaged in secret, dirty, discriminatory practices.

Occasionally they become so confused by what their right and left hands are doing that they stand publicly revealed in the nakedness of their real intellectual dishonesty and prejudice. William Green, in his capacity as president of the American Federation of Labor, reflected the contradictions underlying the noble public position of racial equality so frequently espoused by organized labor. Green began an article written for *The Negro Digest* with, "No philosophy which proclaims the supremacy of any race, color or nationality can square with American principles of freedom and democracy." [3] But in writing these noble sentiments he completely forgot the time some months before when he emerged from an American Federation of Labor executive board meeting in Chicago to be questioned by the press about the policy of the A.F.L. on the Oriental Exclusion Act. In the midst of World War II, while Americans were fighting and dying with the Chinese and while we stood firm for the four freedoms so that the loss of hundreds of thousands of precious American lives would have meaning, Green publicly stated that the American Federation of Labor still supported the Oriental Exclusion Act, and then pontificated, "After all, once a Chinaman always a Chinaman."

[3] "Labor Looks at the Negro," *The Negro Digest* (November 1944), p. 45.

Gunnar Myrdal, whose *An American Dilemma* is a classic study of the Negro in America, summarizes the role of race relations within the American organized labor movements as follows:

The fact that the American Federation of Labor as such is officially against racial discrimination does not mean much. The Federation has never done anything to check racial discrimination exercised by its member organizations.

There is no doubt that the rise in industrial unionism has increased the number of unions which do not discriminate against Negroes.[4]

There are a number of labor unions, mainly within the C.I.O., whose private actions and policy are actually the same as their public program on racial equality. These unions stand as brilliant beacons of hope for democracy. Conspicuous among these unions have been the C.I.O.'s United Packinghouse Workers, Electrical Workers, and the United Automobile Workers. On the whole, however, labor's record on the racial issue is not so far advanced over that of organized business that one can point to organized labor and say unqualifiedly that it is more of a champion than industry in the fight for racial equality and human decency.

It is true that both the A.F. of L. and C.I.O. are, in principle, committed to nondiscrimination. So is the whole American nation. Actually the record has been worse on the union front than in many other fields of American culture.[5]

In spite of the parallel courses of organized business and organized labor, the fault with the American radical is not that he chose to make his bed in the labor movement but that he fell *asleep* in it.

The American radical knows that it is not the whole labor movement itself that is the bride of big monop-

[4] New York: Harper & Bros., 1944, p. 402.
[5] *Ibid.*, p. 792.

oly business, but rather it is the present reactionary
labor leadership with its decadent philosophy which
poisons the entire movement. The radical knows,
and is dead right in his knowledge, that in spite
of the rot in the organized labor movement, it could
represent one of the very best carriers of the democratic hopes and aspirations of the common people.

He knows that the labor movement merely by virtue
of the size of its membership is much more representative than any other organized-interest action group
in the national scene. He knows too that, regardless
of the perversion of labor's principles by an undemocratic leadership, in the last analysis the mass base
and membership can exert a progressive pressure
upon the course of the labor movement. The radical
knows that because of this mass base the interests
and objectives of the organized labor movement can
embrace more of the broad interests and objectives
of the people at large than most other organizations.

In the hands of this radical rests the mission of
democratizing the labor movement. The degree of
democratic participation by all members of the union
in all aspects of union life must be constantly ex-
tended, and the radical must spearhead educational
programs throughout the rank and file of the unions.
The success of these programs will be reflected in basic
changes away from the present conservative, sterile
philosophy of the organized labor movement.

Every man and woman belonging to a labor union
must be educated to understand that in order to improve their lot they must grasp the relationship between their work in the factory, their union, and every
other part of what makes up their whole life. What
does it avail the workingman to fight for a raise in pay
if this raise is accompanied by increased cost of rent,
food, clothing, and medical care? What does it avail
the workingman if his working conditions at the factory are made more healthful but he and his family
are forced to breathe air polluted by those same fac-

tories? The gains workers make through their unions become meaningful not in terms of a few extra dollars in the pay envelope but in terms of what those few extra dollars will do to create a better life for themselves and their families.

When we think of a better life for the worker we must keep clearly in mind the obvious and true picture of the worker as a living man who votes, rents, consumes, breeds, and participates in every avenue of what we call life. The worker as a physical organism is concerned with his health and all matters bearing on it. Adequate medical programs are essential to his welfare and that of his family. As a consumer he buys and wears clothes, buys and eats food, buys and drives automobiles; he is what capital calls the buying and consuming public. As a consumer he is vitally concerned with all economic elements which tend to exploit him, whether misleading advertising, poor quality merchandise, or excessive prices due to monopoly controls. As a human being he has to have a roof over his and his family's heads. Therefore all issues of public versus private housing, and the creation of circumstances where adequate housing can be achieved, become enormously important to him. As a voter the worker finds that every problem in the political arena is his problem. The welfare of many of the organizations with which he is affiliated, including the labor union, depend upon his active and informed political participation. The worker as a parent is deeply concerned about the welfare of his children, their opportunities or lack of opportunities.

Unless the worker is equipped to deal with all of these issues which impinge upon him to constitute a threat to what he has achieved, he finds that after he and his union fight for and succeed in getting a raise in pay, the raise will not be for himself but for his landlord, his grocer, his clothing merchant, his butcher, his baker, and his candlestick maker.

It is ironic that the same American workingman

who recognizes that only through organization and
concerted effort with his fellow employees can he
better his working conditions does not carry on with
organization in dealing with all other problems. Even
the labor union itself adheres to this static, segmental, narrow, warped view in what it calls *straight trade
unionism.* The blinders of *straight trade unionism*
focus all of the worker's attention upon the hourly
pay increase and prevent his seeing what happens to
that money in actual life.

It becomes obvious that the most sacred end for
which the American radical must fight is the development of an over-all philosophy and understanding on the part of the labor movement whereby it
will clearly recognize that the welfare of its constitu-
ents does not depend solely upon an improvement
in economic earnings but upon a general improvement of all of the standards in the life of a worker.
And this can be achieved only by attacking all of the
other problems. It is not just trying to deal with the
factory manager but with every element and aspect,
whether it be political, economical, or social, that
makes up the life of the worker. This will mean a complete change in the philosophy of the labor movement, so that instead of viewing itself as a separate
section of the American people engaged in a separate
craft in a particular industry, it will think of itself as
an organization of *American citizens*—united to con-
quer all of those destructive forces which harass the
workingman and his family. The traditional union
cry of "higher wages and shorter hours" then becomes
one of a wide variety of objectives.

Such a feeling would result in the breaking down
of the segmental differences within our lives whereby
people always "speak in the name of labor," "speak for
business," or "speak for the veterans"—they speak for
every sect, clique, and organization known in this
country, but almost nobody ever "speaks as an American citizen." This sectional, sectarian isolationism

which is so prevalent today in America renders the people more vulnerable to every social ill and—in the end—catastrophe. This is the American form of division. Farmers, workers, businessmen, religious leaders, clerks, all are unable to see beyond their own bailiwick and very few of them recognize that only through seeing the picture of the people as a whole will they be able to work out both the philosophy and the methods of creating a better way of life.

If the organized labor movement cannot stretch to the broad horizon of objectives, it must then help in the building of a broad general People's Organization whose very character would involve an over-all philosophy and attack. In its simplest sense it would be the extension of the principles and practices of organized collective bargaining beyond their present confines of the factory gate. In this kind of People's Organization the organized labor movement, by virtue of its popular constituency, would be an essential element.

The hope of organized labor does not in the last analysis rest in its labor union. It rests in an organized, informed, participating, ever fighting American people.

3

The Crisis

THE CHINESE write the word "crisis" with two characters. One means *danger* and the other means *opportunity*. Together they spell "crisis."

Danger

The danger is the fear of the future. We face the unknown. Man has always unflinchingly faced and advanced upon the worst danger and evils that he knows but will shrink back in uncertainty, confusion, and the deepest fear before the unknown. Whether we like it or not, whether we logically choose to face it or not, the world is increasingly undergoing violent revolutionary upheavals. The world we knew as recently as yesterday is as dead as though it had died a century ago. We know that while certain forms and things of yesterday's world still persist they are nothing but ghosts of the past that will of themselves eventually fade into man's memory and what we call history.

Many people nevertheless long for a return to what used to be. Even with all of its faults they long for it —after all, they were familiar with it. Fear of looking squarely ahead and trying honestly to find out what we can of what lies before us is actually one of the most significant factors in creating the crisis. It is the mass fear of trying to pierce the darkness ahead that paralyzes us into indecision and wretchedness. Unless we face it, inquire into it as far as we can, we will not only be powerless to take a hand in the shaping of our own destiny but may be unable to recognize and exploit new opportunities. Unless we constantly peer forward into the future we will not see the many opportunities the future holds, we will fail to grasp them, and the end will be tragedy. We will miss our greatest chance, our *only* chance, if we continue looking backward instead of forward. To pursue the past is to seek a mirage. The past is dead and men cannot continue as ghosts. It is only in the future that we can live. But we cannot see the light of the future if we deliberately close our eyes and turn our heads.

Let us look at the unknown and see just how unknown it is. Let us see what kind of weapon we are armed with to face the challenge of what is ahead. Surely knowledge and foresight are among our most invaluable weapons, so let us see what we know.

1. We know from the destructive weapons of the atomic age that either we permanently end war or it will most certainly permanently end us.

2. We know from all about us that the democratic way of life is the most efficient instrument that man can use to cut through the barriers between him and his hopes for the future.

3. We know that to date most of our pain, frustration, defeat, and failure have come from using an imperfect instrument—a partial democracy.

4. We know that one of the greatest obstacles in the way of straightening out the affairs of mankind is the confusion and inner conflicts raging within men. It is the vast discrepancy beteen our morals and our practices. It is the human dilemma which constantly draws a shadow of guilt over many of man's noblest endeavors. It gnaws at our vitals and drives us to irrationality.

5. We know that man must achieve faith in himself
—in his fellow man and in his future.

6. We know now that injustice, no matter how
small it may be, is malignant and becomes world-wide
unless checked at once.

7. We know that man must cease worshiping the
god of gold and the monster of materialism. It has
reached the point that man must have spiritual values
if he is to survive physically.

8. We know we must concern ourselves with major
fundamental causes and not with end products.

9. We know we must face the issue of mankind's
obligations as well as its rights. We must recognize
that one of the best ways to insure that men will assume obligations to their fellow men and to society is
to make them feel that they are definitely a part of society and that society means enough to them so that
they actually feel obligated or have obligations.

The world is deluged with panaceas, formulas,
proposed laws, machineries, ways out, and myriads of
solutions. It is significant and tragic that almost
every one of these proposed plans and alleged solutions deals with the structure of society, but none concerns the substance itself—the people. This despite
the eternal truth of the democratic faith that the
solution always lies with the people.

It must never be forgotten that the structure is not
only secondary, but very much so in relation to the
substance. The structure will always be no more
than a reflection of its substance. In the last analysis
of our democratic faith, the answer to all of the issues facing us will be found in the masses of the people themselves, and *nowhere else*.

Let us look at any of our problems. We have said
that we must surely end war or it will surely end us.
It is obvious that if the people of the world are free,
informed, participating to the fullest degree, working together co-operatively, possessed of an understanding of their problems and those of their fellow

men, completely aware of that simple truth that the welfare of one is contingent upon the welfare of all others, secure in a faith in themselves and in their fellow men, committed to ideals of human decency, then there will be no wars.

If, on the other hand, we confine our entire attention to the problem of structure, we will revert to the ancient fallacy of assuming that laws make men rather than that men make laws. The disastrous experience of America's futile attempt to enforce prohibition laws which were contrary to the desires of the masses of the American people is a conspicuous illustration of this type of specious, unrealistic, so-called reasoning.

This, then, is the danger which confronts us as we face the crisis.

Opportunity

As clearly as this danger stands forth, just as clearly does the opportunity present itself. The opportunity is another one of the many chances which have been given to mankind to realize that the hope for the future life is in working with the substance of the world, its people, rather than continued concentration upon its structure. The substance of society is not to be found in a few scattered, rarefied seminars, but in the tremendous masses of struggling, sweating men and women who make up the billions of peoples of the world.

We must devote everything we have to working with our people, not only to find the solution but in order to insure that there will be a solution. The chance to work with the people means the opportunity for the fulfillment of the vision of man. It is the opportunity of a life for mankind of peace, happiness, security, dignity, and purpose. An opportunity to create a world where life will be so precious, worth while, and meaningful that men will not kill other men, will not exploit other men, either economically, politically, or socially; where values will be social and not selfish; where man will not be judged as Christian or non-Christian, as black, yellow, or white, as materially rich or poor, but will be judged as a man. A world in which man's practices will catch up with his ethical teachings and where he will live the full consistent life of practicing what he preaches. A world where man is actually treated and regarded as being created in God's own image, where "all men are created equal." This is the opportunity. Dare we fail?

When we turn our attention to the people we are confronted with one issue. This issue is so deep, so broad, so intense, that it far transcends any of the other problems which we think of as the ills of mankind. It is the one issue toward which we must devote every ounce of our energy, our faith, and our hope. It is the job ahead! It has been the job ahead from time immemorial. It is the awakening of our people from the abysmal apathy that has resulted in the decay and breaking down of a large part of those few ideals which mankind has desperately clung to.

What is this apathy that infects John Smith, American citizen, to the point where in utter frustration, despair, and hopelessness he exchanges life for existence? Let us turn our eyes away from the vast sweeping picture of the masses of people and look for a moment at John Smith. Let us avoid the basic error made by the great majority of studies of people which are filled with statistics and descriptions of everything under the sun, but lack only people, only the human being—John Smith.

How many people have ever thought of the kind of life the average American workingman lives? Not the kind of life he lives when he is unemployed, or on relief, but the kind he lives when he is working. It is a simple life. He gets up on Monday morning and takes his place on the assembly line. He works on the assembly line repeating endlessly over and over again

certain standardized motions. At the end of the week
he comes out of the hell of monotony with a paycheck and goes home to the second round of monotony. If it's the summer he may see a ball game. He may
go to a movie that night or sit around with some
friends in pinochle or poker games. Sunday morning
he is awakened by his wife to go to a church service.
He may spend the afternoon visiting friends here and
there or sitting around, listening to the radio, drinking a little beer, and going to bed. Monday morning
he is back on the assembly line. Life goes on that way,
with certain changes, as the years go by and he wonders what he and his family will do in their old age.
All this time, medical bills and illnesses keep piling up.
His family is increased every so often by a new arrival, with consequent financial worries. That, on the
whole, is his life. A routine in which he rots. The
dreariest, drabbest, grayest outlook that one can have.
Nothing dramatic, nothing exciting, nothing to hope
for, no satisfaction of any desire except in one's own
daydreams. Simply a future of utter despair.

And, to a large extent—why such a future? Why
must life be so drab and dull to the end that it ceases
being life and becomes mere physical existence—not
keeping body and soul together, but just trying to
keep the body together. If the common man had a
chance to feel that he could direct his own efforts,
help to shape the future as well as the present, that
to a certain extent there was a destiny that he could do
something about, that there was a dream that he
could keep fighting for, then life would be wonderful
living.

In our modern urban civilization, multitudes of our
people have been condemned to urban anonymity—
to living the kind of life where many of them neither
know nor care about their own neighbors. They find
themselves isolated from the life of their community

and their nation, driven by social forces beyond their control into little individual worlds in which their own individual objectives have become paramount to the collective good. Social objectives, social welfare, the good of the nation, the democratic way of life— all these have become nebulous, meaningless, sterile phrases.

This course of urban anonymity, of individual divorce from the general social life, erodes the foundations of democracy. For although we profess to be citizens of a democracy, and although we may vote once every four years, millions of our people feel deep down in their heart of hearts that there is no place for them—that they do not "count." They have no voice of their own, no organization (really their own instead of absentee) to represent them, no way in which they may lay their hand or their heart to the shaping of their own destinies. More than a hundred years ago Tocqueville, in his *Democracy in America,* gravely warned the American people of a basic inconsistency in their democratic way of life—an inconsistency which, unless speedily remedied, would probably result in the destruction of democracy. His warning delivered in the year of 1835 is today of the gravest significance:

It must not be forgotten that it is especially dangerous to enslave men in the minor details of life. For my own part, I should be inclined to think freedom less necessary in great things than in little ones, if it were possible to be secure of the one without possessing the other.

Subjection in minor affairs breaks out every day, and is felt by the whole community indiscriminately. It does not drive men to resistance, but it crosses them at every turn, till they are led to surrender the exercise of their will. Thus their spirit is gradually broken and their character enervated; whereas that obedience, which is exacted on a few important but rare occasions, only exhibits servitude at certain intervals, and throws the burden of it upon a small number of men. It is vain to summon a people, which has been rendered so dependent on the central

*power, to choose from time to time the representatives of
that power; this rare and brief exercise of their free choice,
however important it may be, will not prevent them from
gradually losing the faculties of thinking, feeling, and acting for themselves, and thus gradually falling below the
level of humanity.*

*I add that they will soon become incapable of exercising
the great and only privilege which remains to them. The
democratic nations which have introduced freedom into
their political constitution at the very time when they
were augmenting the despotism of their administrative
constitution, have been led into strange paradoxes. To
manage those minor affairs in which good sense is all that
is wanted—the people are held to be unequal to the task;
but when the government of the country is at stake, the
people are invested with immense powers; they are alter-
nately made the playthings of their ruler, and his master
—more than kings, and less than men.*

*It is, indeed, difficult to conceive how men who have
entirely given up the habit of self-government should succeed in making a proper choice of those by whom they
are to be governed; and no one will ever believe that a
liberal, wise, and energetic government can spring from
the suffrages of a subservient people.*

*. . . The vices of rulers and the ineptitude of the peo-
ple would speedily bring about its ruin; and the nation,
weary of its representatives and of itself, would create
freer institutions, or soon return to stretch itself at the feet
of a single master.*

We live in an industrial civilization. Untold material
advancements have been brought to the people by
this civilization. It has brought social enlightenment,
a higher standard of living, and a great extension of
educational and cultural opportunities. But along with
these advantages have arisen forces of so menacing a
character that today they threaten the very foundations upon which rest the hopes of those committed to
the democratic way of life. These destructive forces
are unemployment, decay, disease, and crime. From
the havoc wrought by these forces issue distrust, bigotry, disorganization, and demoralization. Together

they constitute significant indexes of a rapidly growing crisis of confusion in our democratic process. They present a challenge which must be realistically met and solved if the future of democracy is to be secured.

Nowhere today are the stresses, strains, and conflicts of our modern industrial civilization more clearly and dramatically expressed than at the very heart of this civilization—the urban areas. It is here that our people sweat and struggle and suffer. It is here that the rotting of tenements and shacks embraces the body and spirit of men in a cycle of decay. It is here that men hunger for jobs and the right to life—to lift themselves out of the mire of demoralization which now engulfs them. It is here that disheartened, embittered men, tormented by a death agony, strike at their fellow beings with the blind fury of prejudice and hatred. Here disputes between capital and labor have not been "interesting topics" for controversial discussion, but raw, bitter, bloody conflict—the fight for life. Here our basic issues are revealed in all of their ugly nakedness. These warning signs from the heart of our industrial civilization cannot—*must not*—be ignored or evaded.

In these urban areas, as in all areas, people live together in communities. In these communities they, under a democratic society, express their desires and dictates through their own organizations. If we strip away all the chromium trimmings of high-sounding metaphor and idealism which conceal the motor and gears of a democratic society, one basic element is revealed—the people are the motor, the organizations of the people are the gears. The power of the people is transmitted through the gears of their own organizations, and democracy moves forward.

By their own organizations, we mean those organizations in which they participate, which they own, and through which they express their interests, hopes, sentiments, and dreams. These are organizations that are genuinely of the people, by the peo-

ple, and for the people—organizations that by their
very character formulate and articulate a dynamic
democratic philosophy. While it is self-evident that a
disorganized people cannot act as a unit, it is also self-
evident that a people cannot formulate a philosophy
representative of their many diverse loyalties, traditions, and sentiments unless they get together and
through a process of interaction achieve a philosophy
representative of themselves.

It is clear that the existence of these organizations is
vital to the functioning of democracy, for without
them we lack all drive for the development of the democratic way of life. When that drive—the people functioning through their own organizations—is wanting,
the life of our democratic organism comes to a halt.

Democracy is a way of life and not a formula to be
"preserved" like jelly. It is a process—a vibrant, living
sweep of hope and progress which constantly strives
for the fulfillment of its objective in life—the search
for truth, justice, and the dignity of man. There can
be no democracy unless it is a dynamic democracy.
When our people cease to participate—to have a place
in the sun—then all of us will wither in the darkness
of decadence. All of us will become mute, demoralized, lost souls.

A shining illustration of the deep desire of man to
shake off the torpor of frustration, hopelessness, de-
pair, and climb out of the valley of anonymity was
found in the very first meeting, July 14, 1939, of the
first real People's Organization—the Back of the
Yards—which arose in Chicago's notorious stock-
yard section. On that day a People's Congress met and
gave birth to an organization uniting all of the institutions, agencies, power blocs, and interest groups which
made up the life of that community. This People's Organization bridged all of the economic, social, religious, and political cleavages that previously existed

between these groups. The tremendous speed with which the organization developed confirmed the validity of the premises, procedures, and objectives of a People's Organization. Within a period of weeks it attracted the attention and interest not only of national leaders but also of the little people living in small communities throughout the country.

This organization was composed of the people themselves working through their own local organizations. It was created and manned by the people's own indigenous leaders. It included all of the churches, civic, social, athletic, recreational, labor, nationality, and service organizations and many of the businessmen of this community. It embraced a variety of nationalities. The community itself was predominantly Catholic. Once a year the people continued to hold what they call a People's Congress. This People's Congress involves a gathering of delegates from every single organization of the area. At the Congress they elect their officers and formulate their program for the following year, criticize the administration of the past year, decide the finances necessary for the forthcoming program, the means to be used to secure this money, and a host of other problems.

The first Congress presented the appearance of a people's political convention. All of the delegates carried signs with the names of their organizations. The program committee estimated that the volume of business on the agenda would require approximately three hours of discussion and parliamentary procedure. Much to everyone's surprise the People's Congress which had been called to order at 7:30 P.M. was still in full session at 2:00 A.M. This, despite the fact that there had been relatively little disagreement on the issues presented to the convention. The only reason for this interminable delay in completing the business was that in almost every instance when the chairman of a delegation, in response to a roll call, cast the vote of his group, he would find that members of his own delegation challenged the vote. This necessitated the polling of almost every delegation on almost every issue.

The constant repetition of the demand for a polled delegation became exasperating to all of the local leaders until what was actually happening dawned on them. They recognized what by this time was completely obvious: that the average American citizen had been so completely hemmed in and denied the smallest expression or participation in his democracy that when given one of the few opportunities to participate directly in the democratic process he refused to be satisfied with simply sitting in the audience and being referred to by his chairman as a number: "As a chairman of this delegation I cast the vote to be a six yea and three nay." John Smith, the average American, wasn't willing to be identified as simply a "Yea" or a "Nay." John Smith wanted to be called up before the entire convention as part of a polled delegation and, when the chairman said, "How do you, John Smith, cast your vote?" to turn around and face the entire convention, standing on both feet as an American citizen and saying by implication, "I, John Smith, American citizen, a living human being and not just a number but a person who has a part in America and who, by heavens, has got something to say about it, say, 'Yea.'"

This experience was to the local leadership one of the most vivid demonstrations of the emotional starvation of our people for a place in America, for participation, that they had ever experienced. Some of these leaders found themselves deeply moved by the intentness and the eagerness and the hope in the voices and faces of these delegates as they publicly identified themselves and publicly announced *their* decision.

If people are organized with a dream of the future ahead of them, the actual planning that takes place in organizing and the hopes and the fears for the future give them just as much inner satisfaction as does their actual achievement. The kind of participation that comes out of a People's Organization in planning, getting together, and fighting together completely changes what had previously been to John Smith, assembly-line American, a dull, gray, monotonous road of existence that stretched out interminably, into a brilliantly lit, highly exciting avenue of hope, drama, conflict, with, at the end of the street, the most brilliant ending known to the mind of man—the future of mankind.

This, then, is our real job—the opportunity to work directly with our people. It is the breaking down of the feeling on the part of our people that they are social automatons with no stake in the future, rather than human beings in possession of all the responsibility, strength, and human dignity which constitute the heritage of free citizens of a democracy. This can be done only through the democratic organization of our people for democracy. It is the job of building People's Organizations.

We know that this job can be done—it is already well started. The ideas that created the Back of the Yards have spread out—and are still spreading—so that today thousands on thousands of Americans are involved in the building of similar People's Organizations. The People's Organizations built according to the methods and philosophy described above stand today as among the strongest people's groups in the nation. They have been locked in mortal combat with some of the toughest, most securely entrenched power blocs in America and have emerged victorious. They have shown by positive, concrete action, in every field of human endeavor, from housing to food, from wages to health, from child welfare to civic administration, that an organized people can achieve limitless objectives through the democratic process. They are great by their accomplishments, and they glory in the deadly hatred and fear in which they are held by all native nuts.

Part II

The Building of
People's Organizations

4

The Program

THE PRESENT power age defines and evaluates everything in terms of power. To this common and accepted view the field of organization has been no exception. It is universally assumed that the function of a People's Organization is similar to that of any other kind of organization, which is to become so strong, so powerful, that it can achieve its ends. The question as to what constitutes these ends is countered with some general statement like, "Why, the people's program, of course." If we persist in our inquiry as to what is meant by a people's program, raising a series of questions— "Who thought up the program?" "Where did it come from?" "Who worked in its creation?" and other similar queries—we rapidly discover that too often the program is not a people's program at all but the product of one person, five persons, a church, a labor union, a business group, a social agency, or a political club—in short, a program that can be traced to one or two persons or institutions, but not to the people themselves. The phrase "people's program" has become well worn with lip service, but whether such a program actually exists in practice is something else again. The words have become like the word "democracy," a common carrier of so many different meanings that they are meaningless.

Under such circumstances it behooves us to raise the simple question, "What is a people's program?" The question itself leads to the obvious and true answer that a people's program is whatever program the people themselves decide. It is a set of principles, purposes, and practices which have been commonly agreed upon by the people.

What has been completely forgotten and cannot be overemphasized is that a People's Organization carries within it two major functions. Both are equally important. One is the accepted understanding that organization will generate power which will be controlled and applied for the attainment of a program. The second is the realization that only through organization can a people's program be developed. When people are brought together, or organized, they get to know each other's point of view; they reach compromises on many of their differences, they learn that many opinions which they entertained solely as their own are shared by others, and they discover that many problems which they had thought of only as "their" problems are common to all. Out of all this social interplay emerges a common agreement, and that is the people's program. Then the other function of organization becomes important: the use of power in order to fulfill the program.

This does not mean that the organizer cannot state certain general principles during the initial stages of organization. These are general issues of the kind that all people support, such as medical care, full employment, good housing, good schools, equal opportunities, and above all the opportunity to create their own program. The chance to work out their own program will be found to be one of the greatest motivating forces in the building of a People's Organization. This fact in itself bears witness to both the desire of the people to work out their own destiny and the scarcity of opportunities to do so.

But the objective of securing a people's program

absolutely precludes the organizer's going beyond these broad general principles into a detailed blueprint for the future. That kind of program can and must come only from the people themselves. The actual projection of a completely particularized program by a few persons is a highly dictatorial action. It is not a democratic program but a monumental testament to lack of faith in the ability and intelligence of the masses of people to think their way through to the successful solution of their problems. It is not a people's program, and the people will have little to do with it.

There should not be too much concern with specifics or details of a people's program. The program items are not too significant when one considers the enormous importance of getting people interested and participating in a democratic way. *After all, the real democratic program is a democratically minded people*—a healthy, active, participating, interested, self-confident people who, through their participation and interest, become informed, educated, and above all develop faith in themselves, their fellow men, and the future. The people themselves are the future. The people themselves will solve each problem that will arise out of a changing world. They will if they, the people, have the opportunity and power to make and enforce the decision instead of seeing that power vested in just a few. No clique, or caste, power group or benevolent administration can have the people's interest at heart as much as the people themselves.

The working out of a people's program will go hand in hand with the organization of the people. A people's program and the organizing of the people into a people's movement are the opposite sides of the same shield. One cannot be divorced from the other.

Certain universally accepted moral principles will inevitably find their places as cornerstones of any real People's Organization. The very character of the organization will be a social incarnation of that flaming call of the French revolution, "Liberty, Equality, Fraternity," or what the world's great religions describe as respect for "the dignity of man."

Beyond this general statement the organizer is on the kind of ground where even democratic angels fear to tread. If you have faith in the people, you should have faith that they will evolve a people's program. If it is not a program to your liking, remember that it is to their liking. Let all apostles of planning never forget that what is most important in life is substance rather than structure. The substance of a democracy is its people and if that substance is good—if the people are healthy, interested, informed, participating, filled with faith in themselves and others—then the structure will inevitably reflect its substance. The very organization of a people so that they become active and aware of their potentialities and obligations is a tremendous program in itself. It is the ultimate people's program.

Here is the life principle of democratic planning—an awakening in the whole people of a sense of this common moral purpose. Not one goal, but a direction. Not one plan, once and for all, but the conscious selection by the people of successive plans. It was Whitman, the democrat, who warned that "The goal that was named cannot be countermanded." [1]

A People's Organization will inevitably realize that its problems range through every aspect of life. Therefore the program of a People's Organization will be broad, deep and all-inclusive. For this reason a people's program is fundamentally different from the conventional program of the average group that organizes itself into a community council or neighborhood society and purports to be a People's Organization.

These conventional community agency programs

[1] David E. Lilienthal, *TVA—Democracy on the March* (New York: Pocket Books, Inc., 1949), pp. 211–12.

are predicated upon two major fallacies which are conspicuously absent in a people's program. The first basic fallacy of conventional community-council programs is that they view each problem of the community as if it were independent of all other problems. The issues may be youth problems, juvenile delinquency, crime, housing, disease, and a number of others—but the community council comes into existence as an attempt to solve or greatly alleviate *one* of these particular difficulties. The common example is to be found in one of the most frequent programs characteristic of the average community council, that is, the problem of youth or that of delinquency and crime.

From a functional point of view the problem of youth (or any problem) cannot be viewed as an isolated phenomenon. Similarly neither can any specific problem of youth be understood or studied as a problem apart and unto itself. A conspicuous example of this sort of segmental thinking is to be found in our usual studies of delinquency and crime. Crime can properly be viewed only as one facet of a problem of general social disorganization. The opening of the door on the study of crime confronts one with a broad vista of social disorganization. Such aspects of this dreary scene as unemployment, undernourishment, disease, deterioration, demoralization, and many others, including crime itself, are simply parts of the whole picture. They are not separate problems. A sound approach to the field of crime would therefore involve an approach to all of these other problems which are part and parcel of the etiology of crime.

It is very clear that if any intelligent attack is to be made upon the problem of youth or the causes of crime, the community council will have to concern itself with the basic issues of unemployment, disease, and housing, as well as all other causes of crime. This the conventional community council cannot do. It is not equipped to attack basic social issues, and its very character is such that it never was meant to do that kind of job. The community council organized to prevent crime will tell you that its function is in the field of crime purely and it has no place in such controversial fields as conflict between the concept of guaranteed income and welfare, private and governmental housing, public health care and private medical treatment, and other fundamental issues. Intellectually and logically, members of such a council will admit that one cannot hope to attack the causes of crime unless one gets into all the related fields, yet in actual practice they will vigorously abstain from entering any controversial field.

Jobs, higher wages, economic security, housing, and health are some of the important things in life; and they are all controversial. These issues must be met squarely, courageously, and militantly. You don't, you dare not, come to a people who are unemployed, who don't know where their next meal is coming from, whose children and themselves are in the gutter of despair—and offer them not food, not jobs, not security, but supervised recreation, handicraft classes and character building! Yet *that is what is done!* Instead of guaranteeing the right to work for a little bread and butter we come to them with handouts of bats and balls!

To train men for a job when there is no job is like dressing up a cadaver in a full-dress suit; in the end you still have a cadaver.

This same warped outlook applies to a slum community in which the people are living on a low economic level in a life fraught with insecurity. After all, what is a slum? A slum is a dirty, miserable, diseased, human junkyard full of frustration and despair. It is a place where people exist because they do not have the means to live elsewhere. Nobody lives there for any reason except financial pressure or the barriers of race. If a community council tries to do anything significant about any of the problems of the local citizenry, it will find itself faced with the prime objective of attacking those basic elements which make up the economic decay of the slum and its dwellers. If we free ourselves of the shackles of wordiness, the statement of purpose is clear and simple: the job is the unslumming of the slum. This means the battling of all of those forces in the city and the nation which converge to create the human junkyard—worse, the cesspool—known as the slum.

There are those who disagree with this fundamental thesis. They pride themselves on their techniques and talents for adjusting people to difficult situations. They come to the people of the slums under the aegis of benevolence and goodness, not to organize the people, not to help them rebel and fight their way out of the muck—NO! They come to get these people "adjusted"; adjusted so they will live in hell and like it too. It would be difficult to conceive of a higher form of social treason—yet this infamy is perpetrated in the name of charity. Is it any wonder that the men of the slum snarl, "Damn your charity. We want jobs!" But jobs are basic, and the fight for jobs leads one into the most merciless of arenas, the struggle of capital and labor, the fight for life. These issues are fundamental to all others.

The conventional community council—which means practically all community councils—soon discovers that the problems of life are not wrapped up in individual cellophane packages, and because the community council cannot and does not want to get down to the roots of the problems it retreats into a sphere of trivial, superficial ameliorations. The people judge the agency by its program and soon define the agency as insignificant.

The program of a real People's Organization calmly accepts the overwhelming fact that all problems are related and that they are all the progeny of certain fundamental causes, that ultimate success in conquering these evils can be achieved only by victory over all evils. For that reason a people's program is limited only by the horizon of humanity itself.

The kind of static and segmental thinking that regards problems and issues as separate and apart unto themselves logically trips itself into the pitfall of a second fundamental fallacy. It is inevitable that this type of mental isolation, which fails to observe the relationships between problems, would and does lack a pragmatic understanding of the functional relationship between a local community and the larger social scene. It reveals a complete lack of recognition of the obvious fact that the life of each neighborhood is to a major extent shaped by forces that far transcend the local scene.

It requires nothing more than plain common sense to realize that many of the problems in a local community which seemingly have their roots in the neighborhood in reality stem from sources far removed from the community. To a considerable extent these problems are the result of vast destructive forces which pervade the entire social scene. It is when these forces impinge upon the local community that they give rise to a definite community problem. It should, thus, always be remembered that many apparently local problems are in reality malignant microcosms of vast conflicts, pressures, stresses and strains of the entire social order.

The recognition of the functional relationship between a community and the society of which it is a part seems much too obvious to be fortified by illustration. While verbally agreed upon, however, this point has been so ignored in practice that the emphasizing of the obvious is warranted.

A clear demonstration of this functional relationship is to be found in a small industrial town in the Middle West. The economy of this community is centered completely about the packing industry. Outside of the meat-packing plants all the other businesses of the community are of a service character. They are grocery stores, drug stores, laundries, professional services, and others, all catering to the needs of the local people. The residents purchase these services with money earned in the packing companies. This is the kind of community which is popularly known as a "company town."

A glance at the front page of the local paper revealed the basic issues of the community. A substantial part of the front page was devoted to descriptions of grazing conditions and news about cattle out West, and a goodly amount of space was devoted to employment indexes in the Eastern part of the country. In between was a scattering of local news. The newspaper editor, when questioned as to the reasons for a local paper's featuring news of conditions in outlying sections of the nation, responded, "I can tell you why: because it's damn important to us." The most casual observer could not help but recognize the reason for its importance. If grazing conditions out West were poor because of droughts, or if the range was ravaged by an epidemic of cattle disease, fewer cattle would arrive in this community to be butchered. This would mean fewer jobs in the packing industry and, as a result, unemployment in this community. On the other hand, if people in the East became unemployed they would lack the purchasing power to buy meat products. This would result in a reduction of production, with consequent unemployment in the company town. The example is used because it gives a sharply focused picture of the dynamic interrelationship between a community and the general social scene. In other words, the people of the community fully understand that their own welfare and the welfare of their community is dependent upon conditions west and east of their town.

To a very significant extent this interdependence obtains for all other communities. If the automotive workers in Detroit were unemployed they would not be able to buy clothing, electrical appliances, and other products. It then follows that the clothing and appliance industries would curtail production in the face of a reduced market. This would be reflected in fewer jobs in both of those industries. One can pursue the analogy in every kind of community and industry, for social ills are cancerous and do not confine their havoc to single communities or peoples. Although it has taken us a long time to recognize this simple functional relationship in the arena of war and peace, we know now that it is impossible for us to enjoy peace unless the world is at peace; we know that the money spent for defense and war drains off money that could be spent for domestic needs. But we have yet to understand clearly the same tie-up between different economic and social parts of the total system.

The dynamic character of a People's Organization is such that its members recognize the functional relationships that exist between issues, and between their community and the general social structure. They know that their problems are not peculiar to themselves and that their communities do not comprise little isolated worlds. They realize that their local People's Organization has two major objectives: first, to organize and do what can be done on the local scene, and second, to utilize the organization as a springboard for the development of other People's Organizations throughout the nation. They recognize that only through engaging in a national organizational program can they ever hope to break loose from their shackles and their misery. They know that the people elsewhere are the same kind of people, their problems are the same, their needs, their hopes, and their aspirations are the same. A people's program is therefore predicated upon the thesis that only through the combined strength of many organizations such as their own can they ever hope to cope effectively with those major destructive forces which pervade the entire social order and converge upon their communities and themselves to establish the blight that afflicts both the neighborhood and their lives.

5

Native Leadership

THE BUILDING of a People's Organization can be done only by the people themselves. The only way that people can express themselves is through their leaders. By *their* leaders we mean those persons whom the local people define and look up to as leaders. Native or indigenous leadership is of fundamental importance in the attempt to build a People's Organization, for without the support and co-operative efforts of native leaders any such venture is doomed to failure from the very beginning.

These indigenous leaders are in a very true sense the real representatives of the people of the community. They have earned their position of leadership among their people and are accepted as leaders. A People's Organization must be rooted in the people themselves: if a People's Organization were to be thought of as a tree, the indigenous leaders would be the roots and the people themselves the soil. To rest on the soil and be nourished by the soil, the tree must be deeply and well rooted.

To organize the people means to talk with them, to get them together so that they can talk with one another and arrive at a common agreement. But it is obviously impossible to get all of the people to talk with one another. The only way that you can reach people is through their own representatives or their own leaders. You talk to people through their leaders, and if you do not know the leaders you are in the same position as a person trying to telephone another party without knowing the telephone number. Knowing the identity of these natural leaders is knowing the telephone number of the people. Talking with these natural leaders is talking with the people. Working with them is working with the people, and building with them is the building of a People's Organization.

Most attempts at community organization have foundered on the rock of native leadership. The conventional community council has evinced little knowledge or understanding of the significance of indigenous leadership. Such organizations have largely confined themselves to co-ordinating professional, formal agencies which are first superimposed upon the community and subsequently never play more than a superficial role in the life of the community. It is rare to discover a community organization in which the indigenous interest groups and action groups of the community not only participate but play a fundamental role.

Practically all of these community organizations that talk of native leadership think in terms of token representation by community leaders. Even in their token representation one finds residents of the local community but very few, if any, of its leaders. The fact is that almost none of the professional or formal outside agencies that have been active in the field of community organization have any realistic appreciation of the meaning of indigenous leadership. They talk glibly of it but understand and use little of it. If they have accepted local representation, they have generally *selected* persons whom they defined as leaders rather than those persons whom the people have defined and accepted as leaders.

To a certain extent this is a natural, expected reaction. Formal agency representatives who have started community activities have usually regarded themselves as of the "leadership" type. It is the natural egotism of most people to think of themselves in such terms. Therefore when the workers of formal organizations enter a community and search for indigenous leadership they look for persons as similar to themselves as possible. That is one reason why so many of these little organizations known as neighborhood civic committees, community councils, or neighborhood leagues include local people who are of the professional class —doctors, dentists, lawyers, social workers, businessmen and bankers. These types of neighborhood people, usually by virtue of educational background and personal manners, have much more in common with the representatives of the formal agencies than do the rank and file of the area. The organizers themselves feel much more at home with these people, and find them more articulate and more able to talk in terms and values that the outside agency representatives are comfortable with.

Substantially what it amounts to is that the formal agencies' representatives, conceiving of themselves as leaders, hunt for those community persons with whom they can most readily identify. But with rare exception those local professional or business people who are selected by the formal agencies as community leaders may possess a legitimate claim to being native to the communty but no valid claim to being a leader. As to being native to the community, it will often be found that most of them are only half-time natives in that they work within the community and live outside in a more desirable residential area. Furthermore, having very little real relationship with the people (not being part of the people themselves), the actual extent of their being "native" to the community really boils down to their being physically native, whereas on the basis of their thoughts, their aspirations, their hopes, their desires, their sharing the tragedies of the people, these physically native professional and business people are as foreign to the local residents as are outside formal agencies. They have not only never been accepted by the people as leaders, they have never even been thought of in those terms. They possess no following to speak of, and a community council made up of ten of them would in actuality be an organization of ten people—and that's all it would be. It wouldn't even be ten generals and no army, because they are generals only by self-appointment.

Thus it becomes obvious why these alleged community councils very shortly deteriorate into monthly social get-togethers for a small group of professional people who wallow in their egos as self-anointed saviors of the people and commiserate with one another on the poor benighted people of the neighborhood who don't have sufficient intelligence to know what is good for them and ignore this proffered leadership. These community councils soon shrivel up and disappear.

The understanding of what constitutes a genuine native, indigenous leader is rarely found among conventional social do-gooders. The latter are to be found either in professional positions working with various outside agencies or else on the boards of typical community houses. A vivid demonstration of the wide gap in the understanding of leadership between the community people and these outside do-gooders was found in a conference between some of the representatives of the board of a community center and the leaders of the neighborhood People's Organization. The board representatives consisted of economically comfortable persons residing in a good residential section who devoted one evening a month to meeting in the center, where they reviewed all of the purported good that they were doing in the community. This center was represented in the community by a building and nothing more. It did not participate in the life of the community and was not recognized as a neighborhood factor by any of the significant neighborhood groups.

During one discussion some of the leaders of the People's Organization were trying to explain what they meant by native leadership, and they pointed out that those persons holding positions of leadership on the board of the local community center knew very little of the problems of the community and had less real interest in their solution. From the point of view of the People's Organization these outside board members were unknown to the local community, their services were unsolicited, their interest was questionable, and generally their method of doing things *for* rather than *with* the people was resented. So the leaders of the People's Organization inquired as to just what place these outsiders had within the community. (It cannot be too strongly emphasized that when they used the word "outsiders" the People's Organization thought much more in terms of persons whose interests and objectives were outside the community than in terms of geographical location.) At this stage a board member of the local center, a rather young academician specializing in education and personal pompousness, declared, "You people are really isolationists. You don't understand when you talk about leadership or representation just what we represent. We represent the City of Chicago."

This statement convinced the leaders of the People's Organization of the futility of continuing the meeting. Immediately after the meeting they discussed the professor's views:

"Now, that professor says that he and the other guys with him represent the City of Chicago. What the hell are they talking about? When we talk about representing men we really mean representing them. I don't know what they mean by their words. Now take John here [a local labor leader]. When he goes into a factory and organizes the people for his union he says he represents them. He can bargain for them. The employer knows that if John feels that the workers should go out on strike, they will go out on strike—

and if John says they ought to end the strike, they'll go back to work. The boss knows that John really represents the people, but this professor who says he represents Chicago—if he even got into a fight with anybody, who else, outside of his second cousin and maybe a couple of friends of his, would get behind him? Who does he represent? He says, 'the City of Chicago.' What the hell is he talking about? The poor guy, maybe he really believes it. He doesn't mean wrong, he's just nuts!"

Since representatives of formal agencies judge leadership according to *their own* criteria, evaluate what is good or bad in the community according to *their own* standards, and understand life in the community only when interpreted according to *their own* code or standards—it is crystal clear that they don't know the meaning of indigenous leadership, let alone the identities of these natural leaders.

A graphic illustration of natural leadership is to be found in the records of a criminological study made in a slum community. The sociologist making the survey became engaged in conversation with an eleven-year-old newsboy in a slum community in Chicago. This newsboy had seen the sociologist around the neighborhood a good deal and accepted him as somebody living in the community.

SOCIOLOGIST: What do you ever expect to amount to when you grow up?

NEWSBOY: What ya mean?

SOCIOLOGIST: Aw, you know, do you want to be a big businessman?

NEWSBOY: Naw.

SOCIOLOGIST: Do you want to be a big lawyer?

NEWSBOY: Nix.

SOCIOLOGIST: Do you want to be a banker?

NEWSBOY: Why do I want to be a banker?

SOCIOLOGIST: Do you want to be a college professor?

Newsboy: (in an angry tone): Now look here, fella, what do you take me for?

Sociologist: All I'm trying to do is get an idea of just what you expect to be—do you want to be President of the United States?

Newsboy: Naw, I want to be a big shot like Big Butch [notorious leader of a large gang in the community], and have people look up to me and really be a number-one guy.

[Further discussion with the youngster revealed attitudes along this same line.]

Newsboy: Who is the President of the United States anyways? Some guy that Big Butch made President by getting out the vote and paying a buck here and two bucks there. Besides, the President lives some place in Washington, and I don't know the guy. He talks about things like——

Sociologist: Like tariffs, foreign policy——

Newsboy: Yeah, stuff like that. Now Big Butch—he talks our language.

An inquiry among the residents of the community revealed different reasons why Big Butch was regarded as a natural leader. Many of these people were recipients of personal services, financial and other kinds of aid from the conventional social agencies. Their remarks about these agencies threw considerable light on why Big Butch was a natural leader.

"Take my family. If we need dough we go to Big Butch. Tell him about it and he gives over a double sawbuck and no questions asked. It's enough for him to know that we are in trouble. But you go to the Welfare and what happens? They start with how many times a day you part your hair and a hell of a lot of other questions that ain't nobody's business. There are the Smiths down the street. Well, Dottie, who you may have seen here—she's that twenty-year-old good-looking blonde—well, Dottie got into trouble with some guy in the city and the family really needed help. They went to the Welfare but before they could get

the help they had to tell them that Dottie was getting
a kid. Now, you know it ain't decent for other people
to ask those kind of questions. If somebody is in
trouble, they ought to be helped. Well, Big Butch
would never think of poking his nose into anything like
that."

When asked the difference as to the amount of actual help given by both the Welfare and Big Butch it
developed that the Welfare had given the family
about $150 while Big Butch had contributed maybe
$25. The sociologist brought this point up. The news-
boy looked at him with surprise and snorted:

"You don't seem to understand. It isn't what you
give that's so damn important, it's how you give
it. They got that dough from Big Butch not just without a single snoop but with a pat on the back and real
sympathy. When you go to Butch you're a human being. When you go to the Welfare, you're a . . . a . . .
Well, they got a word for it—you're called a 'case.'"

William F. Whyte, in a penetrating analysis of an
Eastern slum community, reported:

*In Cornerville the racketeers are known as free spenders
and liberal patrons of local enterprises. They spend money
in local stores. They patronize the activities of the corner
boys with purchases of blocks of tickets to dances and
with other contributions.*

*One young man in a legitimate business said of T. S.
and his associates: "These gangsters are the finest fellows
you want to meet. They'll do a lot for you, Bill. You go
up to them and say, 'I haven't eaten for four days, and I
haven't got a place to sleep,' and they'll give you something. Now you go up to a businessman, one of the respected members of the community, and ask him. He
throws you right out of the office."* [1]

It is apparent that the primary and most difficult
job confronting an organizer is the actual identification of the local leadership. With few exceptions, the

[1] *Street Corner Society* (Chicago: University of Chicago
Press, 1955), p. 142.

real local leaders are completely unknown outside of the community. Outsiders may know the names of the top local labor leader or banker or businessman, but they rarely know the names of the many little natural leaders who possess a following of twenty or thirty people. Furthermore, ignorance of the identity of the natural leaders of a community is not confined to the outside. Frequently the professional and business people inside the community are not aware of the actual identity of these neighborhood leaders.

The job of locating the individual native leaders is not the kind that lends itself to a formal approach such as questionnaire methods or interviews. It can be done only through a search that requires infinite patience. It means participating in countless informal situations and being constantly alert to every word or gesture which both identifies and appraises the role of certain individuals within the community. It means the closest of observation and constant testing of each clue. The most fruitful setting for the discovery of local leadership is often barroom conversations, poker games, and all other unceremonious get-togethers where the spirit of informality prevails over suspicion and reticence. It means intimate association with particular interest groups within the community—religious, business, social, labor fraternal, and all others. It means working through these interest groups to discover the real leaders. In many cases these leaders will not be officially elected officers, but rather the powers behind the scenes.

. . . I found that in each group I met there was one man who directed the activities of his fellows and whose word carried authority. Without his support, I was excluded from the group; with his support, I was accepted.[2]

Just as people have a variety of interests, so, too, they have a variety of leaders. The problem of identi-

[2] *Ibid.*, p. vi.

fying native leadership is as baffling and complicated as the problem of understanding the forces, interests, and myriad elements that make up the life of a community. A man belongs to a church, a religious society, a fraternal group, a labor union, a social club, a recreational club, a social or political group, and a host of other interest groups. Investigation will disclose that that man looks up to a particular person as a leader, one whose judgment he has confidence in, in political matters, but when he is confronted with a problem of finances he will turn to one of his associates in his fraternal society. And so on down the line. He may have in his orbit of activities five or six individuals to whom he will turn on different matters.

It is obvious then that one rarely stumbles across what might be defined as a complete leader—a person who has a following of forty or fifty people in every sphere of activity. Let us look at it this way. Joe Dokes, a labor steward, may have a following of thirty or forty people who regard his decisions on labor as final. Ten of them, however, if confronted with a financial problem will look to Robert Rowe, who is in an entirely different field of employment and whom they know through their fraternal society. Ten others may look to John Doe, who is a bartender, for financial advice. Of the twenty last mentioned, thirteen may look to Sidney Smith for political leadership; Sidney is a fireman.

And so the question of determining who is a leader involves a large number of partial leaders or leaders of small groups and particularized aspects of their life. The number of natural leaders therefore is considerable. It is as true in that community as it is in any other segment of the population, including that of the reader. These natural leaders—the "Little Joes"—may, it is clear, occupy the most humble roles in the community. A window trimmer may be the president of the Holy Name Society. Or your "Little Joe" may be a garage mechanic, a bartender, an elevator operator, a bus driver. These are the common people and among

them are to be found the small natural leaders of the
natural groups which are present among all people.

One of the most important tasks of the organizer, in
addition to identifying these natural leaders and working with them, is working for their actual development
so that they become recognized by their following as
leaders in more than one limited sphere. This expan-
sion of leadership from a partial role to a more complete one is a natural development that goes hand in
hand with the growth of the People's Organization.

A partial leader soon finds that if he is to retain his
leadership in a People's Organization he must become informed and prove his ability in many of the
other phases that make up the people's program. As
we have seen, the program of a People's Organization
is all-inclusive and embraces every problem in the life
of the people. A leader in such a broad program must
of necessity demonstrate broad abilities and capabilities instead of the limited qualifications which suffice
for a narrow following.

That is what is meant by the development of local
leadership. It does not mean what so many people
think, that there is no leadership among the rank and
file. There is leadership, but it is of the partial variety, and its development is the development of partial leaders into well-rounded leaders of their people.

Even the best outside organizer, one who has
democratic convictions and practices them, who has
complete faith in the people and their leadership, cannot build a People's Organization to a complete structure. He can serve as a stimulus, a catalytic agent,
and render invaluable service in the initial stages of
organization. He can lead in the laying down of the
foundations—*but only the people and their own leaders can build a People's Organization.*

Outside formal agencies that think in terms of going into a community and organizing "democratic"
people's movements are doomed to failure simply because, as their own actions indicate, they fail to grasp

the simplest elements of democracy. On the contrary,
their thinking and actions demonstrate the very antithesis of democracy. In the last analysis their approach and their philosophy represent an anti-democratic intrusion into a democratic community. Gardner
Howland Shaw, once Assistant Secretary of State and
an outstanding exponent of domestic democracy who
devoted a good part of his life to the building of People's Organizations, stated the issue clearly:

*There is nothing in our past or present experience which
suggests that we outsiders can effectively organize . . . a
community to which we do not now and never have belonged. And should a time ever come when it is possible
to effect such an organization, then the character of American life will have so radically changed as to have ceased
to be American. In a large measure it will have become
totalitarian.*

*To be sure, we have established and we can continue to
establish in the underprivileged community a variety of
agencies which we have decided should be of benefit to
that community; and undoubtedly some if not all of these
agencies will benefit to a certain degree some of the members of that community. . . . We can also establish these
agencies in haphazard and competitive fashion, as we have
often done in the past, or we can plan for their effective
utilization with as much intelligence as possible through
some sort of procedure of co-ordination, as we have done
on occasions more recently. But, whether the agencies are
established or not established, and whether they compete
with each other or are co-ordinated, the fact remains that
the community is not being really organized either by us
or by the people living within its confines. Essentially what
we are doing is to decide what is good for the underprivileged area without any real participation by, or even
sustained consultation with, the people of that area; we
are trying to do something to rather than with it. In the
last analysis, our approach is fundamentally authoritarian,
fundamentally undemocratic.*[3]

[3] *Fighting Delinquency from Within.* Address delivered before the New York State Conference of Social Work, Rochester,
New York, November 16, 1944. Published by the Welfare Council of New York City.

6

Community Traditions and Organizations

The foundation of a People's Organization is in the communal life of the local people. Therefore the first stage in the building of a People's Organization is the understanding of the life of a community, not only in terms of the individual's experiences, habits, values, and objectives, but also from the point of view of the collective habits, experiences, customs, controls, and values of the whole group—the *community traditions*.

To a significant degree people express their traditions through their local organizations. The form, the character, and the purpose of all the local agencies reflect the traditions of the community. Agencies will be found representing almost every facet of the life of the community: religion, labor, business, social, fraternal, recreational, service, nationality, and many others.

In the building of a Peoples Organization the agencies and local traditions are to an important extent the flesh and blood of the community. It is impossible to overestimate the importance of knowledge of the traditions of those people whom it is proposed to organize.

This does not mean that one has to have a complete

knowledge of all their traditions, but it does mean that the organizer should have a familiarity with the most obvious parts of a people's traditions. And it does mean more than the organizer's recognition that he does not go into an Orthodox Jewish community with a ham sandwich.

Many organizers will speak of the difficulties of trying to overcome local traditions and local taboos in creating a people's movement. One should be constantly on guard, however, against attacking local traditions. After all, if the organizer believes in democracy and is concerned with what Jefferson referred to as "a decent respect to the opinions of mankind" there is no reason to oppose or try to break down local traditions. Furthermore, this course of activity only leads to hostility, conflict, and the creation of an impossible condition for a real People's Organization.

Those who build People's Organizations begin realistically with what they have. It does not matter whether they approve or disapprove of local circumstances, traditions, and agencies; the fact remains that this is the material that must be worked with. Builders of People's Organizations cannot indulge in the sterile, wishful thinking of liberals who prefer to start where they would like to begin rather than with actual conditions as they exist.

We move step by step—from where we are. Everyone has heard the story of the man who was asked by a stranger how he could get to Jonesville; after long thought and unsuccessful attempts to explain the several turns that must be made, he said, so the anecdote runs: "My friend, I tell you; if I were you, I wouldn't start from here." Some planning is just like that; it does not start from here; it assumes a "clean slate" that never has and never can exist.[1]

The starting of a People's Organization is not a matter of personal choice. You start with the people, their traditions, their prejudices, their habits, their atti-

[1] David E. Lilienthal, *TVA—Democracy on the March* (New York: Pocket Books, Inc., 1949), p. 213.

tudes, and all of those other circumstances that make up their lives.

It should always be remembered that a real organization of the people, one in which they completely believe and which they feel is definitely their own, must be rooted in the experiences of the people themselves. This is essential if the organization is to be built upon and founded upon the people.

The traditions of a people are interwoven in the fabric of their experiences. To understand the traditions of a people is not only to know their prejudices, beliefs, and values, but to understand them. It is to ascertain those social forces which argue for constructive democratic action as well as those which obstruct democratic action.

To know a people is to know their religions. It is to know the values, objectives, customs, sanctions, and the taboos of these groups. It is to know them not only in terms of their relationships and attitudes toward one another but also in terms of what relationship all of them have toward the outside. An excellent illustration of the importance of understanding community mores and of the difficulties that arise from lack of knowledge of local traditions, is contained in the following organizer's report:

"The last People's Organization I worked with was primarily Catholic. The Catholics are not hidebound on a lot of things; as a matter of fact, whenever I would visit with a priest, why, it was pretty customary for him to offer me a Scotch and soda or a highball. Not only that, but at church carnivals they have all kinds of gambling games and even slot machines. Gambling and drinking were not regarded in the neighborhood by anybody, including the churches, as being immoral or something to be frowned upon. The only time gambling or drinking was really condemned was if it was carried to excess, such as a guy getting drunk frequently or else blowing enough of his paycheck on the horses so that his family had a tough time the next week. Everybody in the neighborhood—and that includes the parish church, too—had a pretty sensible and reasonable point of view on drinking and gambling.

"Well, after eight months in that kind of community I found myself down in Oak Root trying to build a People's Organization. Oak Root is not only a Protestant community, but most of the Protestants are fundamentalists. I made the bad mistake of not familiarizing myself with traditions, religions, and the way the people live, and the next thing I knew I was up to my neck in hot water. I found that a number of the ministers were openly charging me with being an 'immoral and depraved creature of the Devil.' Before I could get over the shock of surprise I discovered that the facts that they were presenting in support of their charge were accepted by most of the people. After hearing the facts and learning a little bit about community traditions, I pleaded guilty and faithfully promised never to repeat my 'immoral and depraved' behavior (at least not in the vicinity of Oak Root). I was guilty of being, in the words of one of the ministers who was most zealous in prosecuting me, 'the man seen entering the Platinum' (a large motion picture theatre in a nearby Big City). The act of entering a movie house to 'witness a lewd and lascivious performance by a brazen, half-undressed female was considered a flagrant violation of a community built around religious institutions which condemn the witnessing of a motion picture as a 'mortal sin.'"

Communities differ in moral standards according to their customs. Another example of the difference in definitions of moral values between moral leaders of the community and an outside moralist is to be found in the statement of a leading priest in one community: "These Welfare people from the outside always get upset when they are working with a family and they find out that the husband comes home smelling of liquor. They should know that a man working in the cooling rooms of the packing plants—who has been frozen most of the day—when he gets through working he wants to get warmed up a little, so he takes a drink or two. It's only natural and human and it's nothing to get all upset about like these Welfare workers do."

Differences among groups must also be carefully studied and understood. Each group is bound by ties of tradition, common experience, and ethnic identification. In some cases the traditions, attitudes, and customs of first- and second-generation Americans are carry-overs from the Old World. It is important to know the traditions of these groups not only on an intramural basis but also in terms of their relationships with other ethnic groups. A wide variety of social distances will be revealed between one ethnic group and others. Slavs will feel closer to each other than to the Irish. The preponderant ethnic groups will be in sharper competition with each other than with the smaller neighborhood groups. As a result hostilities and jealousies may be more bitter among the major groups. Agnes E. Meyer, reporting on conditions existing in a Chicago community prior to the building of a People's Organization, wrote:

Though all these people sweated—or froze—side by side in the packing houses, they ignored each other in the streets, when not engaged in open feuds. The priests were not on speaking terms and passed each other without salutations. Language barriers increased the tension. The Lithuanians favored the Poles as enemies, the Slovaks were anti-Bohemian. The Germans were suspected by all four nationalities. The Jews were generally abominated and the Irish called everyone else a "foreigner." No Negro was safe in Packingtown on his way to work from his Southside quarters. When the Mexicans invaded this cheap labor market, they were treated worse than the Negroes.[2]

Ethnic groups express their ethnic character not only through lodges and social and fraternal organiza-

[2] "Orderly Revolution," *Washington Post*, June 4, 1945.

tions but in many instances through their religious organizations. This is true of Protestants, Jews, and Catholics. There are still in America a great many of what are called nationality churches among the Catholics. There is a Lithuanian Catholic church, a German Catholic church, a Slovak Catholic church, a Polish Catholic church, and others. These ethnic groups banded together after arriving in this country and created little Polands, little Germanys, little Slovakias, and little Lithuanias, which included churches of their own. In many of these nationality churches all of the sermons are given in the native tongue.

The standards, the codes, the attitudes, and the patterns of the local people touch every part of their life, even their food habits. Local leaders, in describing the wide gaps existing between outsiders and the local people, comment:

"Why, during the depression when Welfare workers came down among our Italian people, they would give them a certain amount of money to spend each week and some education on what they called 'nutrition' so they could get the most food for their money. These Welfare workers would get upset because our Italian families insisted on buying very good olive oil to cook with. Anybody ought to know that Italians have to have olive oil to cook with and it's something much more important than budgets or stuff like that.

"The same thing happened with some of our Jewish families. Some of the Welfare workers began screaming about the Jewish families on relief buying chicken on Friday. Well, our Jewish families have said all along, and we believe them, that they've just got to have a piece of chicken for Friday night, so if they're willing to sacrifice other things for the sake of having chicken, that's their business and it ain't that of the Welfare workers.

"You know, there are a lot of outsiders that make bad mistakes on this food business. Now, I had a teacher who came into a public school and in one of her talks to the kids she said, 'Now we are going to learn how to eat good things that have vitamins in them and stuff like that and not be old-fashioned and ignorant and things like that and not just eat spaghetti and things like that.' That teacher never knew why she got slugged on the way home. She should have known that she was insulting the families of all the kids and was really calling them ignorant."

Another example of conflict in values between outsiders and the local people is found in the following description of the local reaction toward a recreation project that had been sponsored in Greenwich Village:

Even in athletics, money counted quite as much as the game. It was the regular thing to put up bets on every game, whether it was a scratch game between two block teams or the finals of a city-wide tournament, the winning team receiving the pot. The amount put up varied all the way from five cents to fifty dollars. It was striking evidence of the readiness to put up money in a gamble, but not to spend it directly for a recreation, that when one of the local centers attempted to run an interblock punch-ball contest, a sufficient number of teams were not willing to pay the very small entrance fee to make possible the purchase of a trophy and other minor expenses of running off the tournament. These same teams were ready to put up much larger sums on the chance of their team's winning these sums back, along with a corresponding amount put up by the opposing team.[3]

The important thing here is that trophies, statues, medals, and things like that have very little meaning to boys who are coming up the hard way in the streets and who have accepted the gold standard and codes of a materialistic society. Recognition is not in terms of statues to put over the fireplace (if you have a fireplace) but how much money you have in your pocket.

Another contrast between local traditions and out-

[3] Caroline F. Ware, *Greenwich Village* (Boston: Houghton Mifflin, 1935), p. 147.

side standards was illustrated by a report on a social affair of a People's Organization in Chicago:

Most successful from the standpoint of attendance was the Jungle Jamboree, a large dance held in a rented hall [in the spring]. Every affiliated organization worked feverishly to promote the affair, which had the secondary purpose of raising money for the council's work. Hundreds turned out to what proved to be a pretty boisterous party. The news that a bar was set up in the hall came as a shock to social workers who, for a long time, had been attempting to raise standards in the community. But the people Back of the Yards have never been noted for being tee-totalers, and since the Jamboree was their own party they prepared it as an affair they expected to enjoy.[4]

That organizer who has a grasp and understanding of local traditions is able to organize with a rapidity and stability which is astounding to observers.

"Across the Tracks" had always been known for its toughness. Many of the residents of that community resented the fact that the moment that they identified themselves as being from Across the Tracks they were automatically regarded as ruffians who would start a fist fight at the drop of a hat. The same definition was openly made by employment agencies when an Across the Tracks resident filed an application for a job. This tradition was used in an organizational campaign in a positive sense so that the people's movement that arose out of this community gloried in its toughness. The tradition carried the campaign through to an unbroken series of victories against some of the most powerful vested interests of its city.

In Bagville there was a legend that the area had been a very healthy, prosperous, and attractive community until 1915, when a disastrous flood brought havoc and wreckage to it. Since that flood the area had become notorious as one of the worst slums of the country. The beauty of the pre-flood Bagville became

[4] Kathryn Close, "Back of the Yards," *Survey Graphic*, December 1940.

a goal of the community—although many of the residents were too young to remember the flood—incorporated in a slogan to rising Bagville: "Back to Where It Was Before the 1915 Flood." This slogan was a rallying point for many of the diverse elements of the community and a motive driving force in the organization of a People's Movement.

In all communities there are multiple agencies and organizations—ranging from churches, athletic groups, nationality associations, benevolent orders, religious societies, women's clubs, labor unions, businessmen's groups, service organizations, recreation groups, fraternal societies, lodges, political parties, to a host of other organizations. When organizational work starts, it can be safely assumed that a great many of these agencies will be antagonistic toward the development of a People's Organization. They will express their hostility in many forms, such as disagreement with the program, concern for the future possibilities of this kind of organization, and every reason but the real reason. The real reason is that these agencies have a stake in the life of that community. Many of them are in constant competition with the others and engaged in an unceasing struggle for survival. They define the introduction of a new movement as a further threat to their security. It means that many of their own people will share their allegiance with this new organization. It means also that this new organization will tap community resources for funds, thereby diminishing the amount of money available to the already existing agencies. Likewise, existing agencies fear that some of their own functions will be absorbed by the new organization and that their own survival will be further jeopardized. Still another reason for resentment is the fact that the coming in of a new organization carries with it the implication that the local organizations have not done their job or are incapable of doing it.

In one community a minister said to an organizer: "Why shouldn't I feel bitter about your coming in here? When this community says that they are going to put an end to this and to that, it really means that I have been sitting here for the last twelve years not doing anything and if they succeed in doing it, it's going to make me look like more of a fool, and what are my contributors going to say next year when I ask them to give support to my church? They are going to say, 'Well, look what this People's Organization has done in just one year and you have been telling us for all these years that nothing could be done about it.'"

The essence of the situation is that the existing community agencies will generally be resentful and hostile toward a new organization because that organization is to all apparent purposes a basic threat to their own identity and security.

Many organizers become embittered by the obstacles placed in their path by the local organizations and they fail to recognize that they themselves are partly at fault. In their fervor they assume functions which are regarded by a local agency as its own property. The organizers may defend themselves by saying: "After all, that church says that this kind of program is what they are doing, but they haven't done anything about it and it needs doing and that's why we are doing it. We wouldn't go into it if they were carrying their part of the load, but we are not taking anything away from them because they never did anything about it before." The organizer should recognize that the local organizations with whom he is having difficulty are a most significant part of the democratic way of life. That to a strong degree they represent the very skeleton of democracy.

Democracy is that system of government and that economic and social organization in which the worth of the individual human being and the multiple loyalties of that individual are the most fully recognized and provided for. Democracy is a system of government in which we recognize that all normal individuals have a whole series of loyalties—loyalties to their churches, their labor unions, their fraternal organizations, their social groups, their nationality groups, their athletic groups, their political parties, and many others.

Democracy provides for the fulfillment of the hopes and loyalties of our people to all of the various institutions and groups of which they are a part. It is not a single, unqualified, primary loyalty to the state, as the totalitarians would have it—a loyalty in which all other institutions and organizations are completely swept out of the picture. Under totalitarianism, you may be loyal to your church if your state decrees that you may be. But it is a loyalty by sufferance of the state.

The organizer would have far fewer difficulties with the local agencies if he fully understood the reasons for their resentment. Once he understood the reasons he would first of all work *with all of the agencies of the community* to build a People's Organization of which they were the very foundation. The People's Organization would take the initial form of an organization of organizations. That kind of organization does not present a threat to any one individual agency. On the contrary, through a People's Organization and the co-operative relationships that are part of it, the walls of isolation separating the various agencies are broken down. Intimate association and frank conversations will and do destroy those prejudices and suspicions which result in agencies fighting each other instead of working together. A local priest who in the early stages had opposed the building of a People's Organization said:

"In the beginning I was really afraid that this new People's Organization would reduce even more the already small financial support which all of our local agencies and churches received from the people. Whenever I had a bazaar, all of the other churches and organizations would keep their people away from my bazaar because they didn't want them to spend their money at my place. They, of course, hoped that the people would spend their money only at their own churches. I suppose it was a natural desire to conserve the financial resources of their own people. Now, however, since the People's Organization came into being, whenever our people think of themselves they think of all the people, all the agencies, and all of everything that makes up the whole neighborhood. Until the People's Organization came my bazaar never made more than four thousand a year. Since the People's Organization, we have never made less than twenty-two to twenty-five thousand a year. There are some people who think only in terms of figures. They say, 'We are not interested in words but in dollars and cents.' Well, in straight dollars and cents the figures speak for themselves. Now when I have a bazaar everybody, and that means every other church, too, supports our bazaar. They encourage their people to come to ours, just as we encourage our people to go to their bazaars. It is really amazing how much more there is in life and for everybody if we all pull together instead of cutting each other's throats."

Furthermore, being built right up from the roots of the community, a People's Organization is not an outside movement coming into the community. The purpose of the organization should be interpreted as proposing to deal with those major issues which no one single agency is—or can be—big enough or strong enough to cope with. Then each agency will continue to carry out its own program, but all are being banded together to achieve sufficient strength to cope with issues that are so vast and deep that no one or two community agencies would ever consider tackling them. This kind of program does not present any menace to the future or reflection upon the past of any local agencies.

Frequently, however, the organizer will encounter

various community agencies whose policies are antagonistic toward the basic ideas of a People's Organization. In such cases he will not be discouraged or reflect the hostilities of these agencies if he remembers that just as people change when they get to know each other, so do the policies of community agencies change once these agencies become involved in the People's Organization. If the leaders of community agencies get to know the leaders of other community organizations, their personal opinions and attitudes are altered, with a consequent change in the attitudes and policies of their respective organizations. With this clearly in mind the organizer need not be too concerned at the start about the reactionary policies of individual community agencies. He will find that a mixture of the progressive policies of a progressive People's Organization and the individual conservative policies of a conservative neighborhood agency will result in a progressive product. Experience has shown this to be true no matter how wide a gap previously existed between the two agencies. It is like the chemical process in which hydrogen and oxygen, brought together in proper proportions and under the right conditions, result in an entirely new product—water. It becomes the job of the organizer first to get the two elements together and second to make sure that they are brought together in the proper proportions.

That kind of approach is actually the only kind that would be truly representative of the people and truly in keeping with the spirit of democracy. A People's Organization actually *is* built upon all of these diverse loyalties—to the church, to the labor union, to the social groups, to the nationality groups, to the myriad other groups and institutions which comprise the constellation of the American way of life. These loyalties combine to effect an abiding faith in, and a profound loyalty to, the democratic way of life.

7

Organizational Tactics

THE MOTIVES of the American radical engaged in organizational work will be viewed by many people and organizations with suspicion, cynicism and hostility. They will measure him with the only measuring stick that a materialistic society has taught them, one that is marked in units of selfishness, exploitation, money, power, and prestige. They will wonder and ask, "What's in it for him?" "What's his angle?" "What's his cut?" "There must be a catch in it some place—what is it?" "People don't do things for nothing—what's he doing it for?"

Basically, the radical must meet this opposition by a simple honesty, and must always remember that in the long run he is striving to make honesty a virtue instead of a stigma of stupidity. One of the most significant ways that he can do this is by the power of personal example.

Most suspicion of him will change to skepticism, then to incredulity—and finally to acceptance. In reaching a mass judgment of the motives of the organizer, the people will of course have to rely mainly on his words and actions. To the people, the radical's actions will be by all odds the central part of the picture, and his words the background.

Throughout the organizational period many people and organizations will revert to avarice, individualistic opportunism, personal exploitation, and lack of faith. The radical must never permit these reversions to embitter or frustrate him to a point where he loses faith in the people and begins to be "disillusioned." The radical does what he does because of his love for his fellow men and there is nothing more heart-breaking than having one's offer of love rejected. Consequently some who have undergone this crushing experience have emerged cynical, faithless—individuals who repudiate the masses of people, regarding them only as stupid puppets to be manipulated for personal aggrandizement. This is one of the reasons why some Socialists, rejected in their efforts, later became Fascists.

This sorry course of events cannot happen in the case of the real radical. The radical cannot suffer *personal* defeat because in a sense he is selfless. In part he lives the kind of philosophy expressed in Schiller's words: "Know this, a mind sublime puts greatness into life, yet seeks it not therein." The radical fights not for himself but for ideas, and ideas have a way of living on—they don't kill as easily as man, and he knows that in the end the best ideas or way of life will prevail.

The radical's affection for people is not lessened, nor is he hardened against them even when masses of them demonstrate a capacity for brutality, selfishness, hate, greed, avarice, and disloyalty. He is convinced that these attitudes and actions are the result of evil conditions. It is not the people who must be judged but the circumstances that made them that way. The radical's desire to change society then becomes that much firmer. Each blow makes him a stronger radical. He thinks of the people precisely as did that great radical Thomas Paine. He remembers Paine's defense of the common people, in *Rights of Man,* against the vicious attack of Edmund Burke. Burke had furiously assailed the people of France and their barbaric behavior in cutting off the heads of those who opposed the Revolution and carrying the heads triumphantly through the streets on spikes. Paine replied to Burke:

Their heads were stuck upon spikes, and carried about the city; and it is upon this mode of punishment that Mr. Burke builds a great part of his tragic scene. Let us therefore examine how men came by the idea of punishing in this manner.

They learn it from the governments they live under, and retaliate the punishments they have been accustomed to behold. The head stuck upon spikes, which remained for years upon Temple Bar, differed nothing in the horror of the scene from those carried about upon spikes at Paris; yet this was done by the English government. It may perhaps be said that it signifies nothing to a man what is done to him after he is dead; but it signifies much to the living: it either tortures their feelings, or hardens their hearts; and in either case, it instructs them how to punish when power falls into their hands.

Lay then the axe to the root, and teach governments humanity. It is their sanguinary punishments which corrupt mankind. . . . The effect of those cruel spectacles exhibited to the populace, is to destroy tenderness, or excite revenge; and by the base and false idea of governing men by terror, initial of reason, they become precedents.

Radicals are not repelled by moral malignancy and evil in people, but on the contrary regard with wonder the fact that the masses of people, subjected to the kind of society in which they live, should retain so much decency and dignity. The radical constantly finds his faith in man fortified. He recognizes that a certain amount of petty larceny in the personality is a normal human secretion among people constantly being squeezed by the larcenous pressures of a materialistic society. He realizes that the people of today live in a system that places the highest premium on personal possessions and regards material poverty as failure. It is a system within which, with few exceptions, the material ends justify the means. Morality is for words and not for work.

In a survey of American educational institutions Robert M. Hutchins, then President of the University of Chicago, developed the thesis that the character of our educational systems reflects the character of the society that sustains and engenders them. The society in this instance is one characterized by aggression, both individual and social, by a wide disparity of wealth, privilege, and opportunity, by materialistic values and standards, and by a rather confused and demoralized ideology. Our educational system is the inevitable progeny of its present society. Hutchins continued with this statement:

A further consequence of American ideals in American education is that moral questions are omitted from it. The end given is money. The issue is how to obtain it as rapidly as possible and stay out of jail.[1]

People living under a selfish system become adjusted to it in order to survive. They therefore naturally acquire a personal selfishness and just as naturally assume the same selfishness exists in all others, including the organizer. This ingrained suspicion must be destroyed; its destruction is an essential part of the fight for a people's world. Not only must the dignity of the individual be restored but in that process man must begin to see the good in other men. *He cannot see the good in others unless he has some of it within himself.*

The radical, with full recognition that many of our people are warped by the kind of society of which they are products, will realize that in the initial stages of organization he must deal with the qualities of ambition and self-interest as realities. Only a fool would step into a community dominated by materialistic standards and self-interest and begin to preach ideals. Only a fool would try to persuade people to cross a river without first having either boats or a bridge. Rad-

[1] Robert M. Hutchins, "Ideals in Education," *American Journal of Sociology* (July 1937), p. 8.

icals, contrary to public opinion, are not fools. Although they have been regarded and condemned as crackpots and crowned with the vilest of opprobriums, the history of man has vindicated them as the wisest of the wise.

The radical recognizes that in order to work with people he must first approach them on a basis of common understanding. It is as simple and essential as learning to talk the language of those with whom one is trying to converse. The procedures or tactics that follow from here on should be understood in those terms. They are the simple means with which to arouse people to stand up and move. Some critics have described these means as fighting fire with fire. This is not strictly true, because these procedures are used only during the early stages of organizational activities. The radical is fully conscious of the fact that they are temporary expedients for the beginning of the organization. They are the instruments used in preparing the scaffolding for the building of an environment which will permit people to express their innate altruism. After the organization is soundly built, they will work co-operatively for reasons of social good rather than individual interest.

Practically all people live in a world of contradictions. They espouse a morality which they do not practice. They will tell you that they fervently believe in Christianity and the brotherhood of man and all of its moral implications in spite of the fact that a majority of their actions are designed to exploit their fellow men. They find themselves constantly trying to extricate themselves from this dilemma by erecting a ladder of rationalization such as, "Sure, we believe in Christianity, but after all business is business." The vast separation between their moral standards and actual ways of living resolves itself into extraordinary inconsistencies and inner conflict.

This dilemma can and should be fully utilized by the organizer in getting individuals and groups involved in a People's Organization. It is a very definite Achilles' heel even in the most materialistic person. Caught in the trap of his own contradictions, that person will find it difficult to show satisfactory cause to both the organizer and himself as to why he should not join and participate in the organization. He will be driven either to participation or else to a public and private admission of his own lack of faith in democracy and man. Most people are eagerly groping for some medium, some way in which they can bridge the gap between their morals and their practices. The failure to find a satisfactory and viable way to resolve this inner conflict leads to the rationalization that "whatever is, is right," and can't be changed. It is the old story that once you accept a false premise you must continue to sustain it by additional false arguments. Once you tell a lie you are going to have to tell another to cover up the first and an indefinite cycle has begun. A Christian who believes that man was created in God's own image but nevertheless retains his prejudice against Negroes will resolve his inner struggle by rationalizing that Negroes are "really inferior." Man must be provided with an opportunity for a healthy, consistent reconciliation of morals and behavior or he will be forced into a pathology of rationalization.

Many exponents and supporters of People's Organizations bitterly denounce self-interest as one of the main obstacles that must be crushed if people are to be organized into a co-operative fellowship. Both liberals and organizers have attributed the failure of their attempts to the rampant spirit of individualism and selfishness. These organizers have never appreciated that many seeming obstacles can be utilized to great advantage. The fact is that self-interest can be a most potent weapon in the development of co-operation and identification of the group welfare as being of greater importance than personal welfare.

In approaching people the shrewd organizer will

not stand back in sackcloth and ashes and mourn certain phases of life or traditions as obstacles to his work. It should be remembered as a maxim in community organization that every obstacle contains certain assets.

Certainly the element of self-interest has been constantly condemned as one of the large obstacles in the development of an esprit de corps. Such self-interest is based a good deal on the law of the jungle, and certainly the survival of the fittest does not lend itself to thinking and acting according to co-operative and self-sacrificing for-the-other-guy philosophy. Yet this seeming obstacle can be and has been used as one of the most driving motive forces in the development of a co-operative organization. A vivid example of the use of greed for good is revealed in the experiences of a successful organizer.

"We had just gotten started in this neighborhood and gotten some of the organizations together when I went to see Mr. David. Mr. David was a businessman who had been in the fruit and vegetable business in this community for many years. Throughout this period he had avoided participation in any kind of social-betterment program or community group. He was in many respects a typical businessman of the community. I told him that we were starting a community organization to do something about many of the problems of the neighborhood, including many of the neighborhood children who were underfed, miserably clothed and rapidly drifting into delinquency. Throughout my conversation with Mr. David he kept one hand in his right-hand trouser pocket, where he was obviously fingering paper money, and his eyes wandered around the store. His whole manner let me know that in his opinion I was just another 'do-gooder' and as soon as I finished my song and dance he would give me a dollar or two and wish me well. I suddenly shifted from my talk on the children and began to point out indirectly the implications of his joining our organization. And then it happened. His eyes lit up like a pair of neon lights and you could almost see the cogwheels turning around in his head like a Disney cartoon and his thoughts were audible to the point of needing no verbal amplification. As I said, I could almost hear Mr. David thinking: 'Why, this is wonderful! I'll go to this meeting and get up before all of those labor leaders, ministers, priests and heads of these different nationality organizations and I'll say: "For years my heart has been bleeding to see the poor children of our neighborhood going around the way they have and for all these years I have not been able to do anything because there was never a real People's Organization—right from this neighborhood. Oh, it's true, that there were a lot of well-meaning people who would come in, but they didn't know what it was all about and they really didn't care for the people here. You know that too. And so there was little that I could do, but now—now that the people themselves have gotten together and now that I have somebody I can work with, my heart is breaking with happiness and I, Joseph David, want to help this organization not only with money but with anything you want and I will therefore give three hundred dollars to this movement."

" 'And where could I get better business relations than at this meeting. I can't get advertising like this. Why, whenever somebody is out shopping and meets his labor leader, minister, priest, rabbi, president of the bowling club, he will be told right away to buy his vegetables from me. They will say, "Go to David's. David is a fine fellow. He is interested in more than just his business. He is part of us, working and fighting with us." It's wonderful!'

"Then David turned to me and said, 'I'll be at that meeting tonight.' Immediately after I left David I went across the street to Roger, who is in the same business, and I talked to him the same way. Roger had a doubled-barreled incentive for coming. First there was David's purpose and secondly Roger wanted to make sure that David would not take away any part of his business.

"That night at the meeting we had what you would certainly call a couple of unsocial characters. That is, they were not one bit interested in the welfare of the local people. Their sole interest lay in getting as much advertising, good will, and—finally—as much business as possible. They were present to make a commercial investment.

"During the course of the meeting both David and Roger got up and made talks right along the lines which had been so obvious in their thinking processes of that afternoon. They both made generous contributions. Since they expressed such a deep interest in the welfare of our children we appointed them to the Children's Committee. Again I felt I could guess their reaction: 'Well, I did what I came for, but now they've put me on this committee so I will go along for a couple of meetings and then I will step out of the picture. After all, I should spend my life on committees!'"

As part of their first assignment the members of the committee were sent into some of the West Side tenements of the neighborhood. There Roger and David personally met the children who had been the subjects of their orations. They met them face-to-face and by their first names. They saw them as living persons framed in the squalor and misery of what the children called "home." They saw the tenderness, the shyness, and the inner dignity which are in all people. They saw the children of the neighborhood for the first time in their lives. They saw them not as small gray shadows passing by the store front. They saw them not as statistical digits, not as impersonal subjects of discussion, but as real human beings. They got to know them and eventually a warm human relationship developed. Both Roger and David came out of this experience with the anger of one who suddenly discovers that there are a lot of things in life that are wrong. One of them was violent in his denunciations of the circumstances that would permit conditions of this kind to go on unabated. Today these two individualists are the foremost apostles of co-operative organization.

If they had been originally asked to join on grounds of pure idealism they would unquestionably have rejected the invitation. Similarly if the approach had been made on the basis of co-operative work they would have denounced it as radical.

Just as individualism and self-interest can be transformed from an obstacle into an advantage, so can the spirit of competition be used to develop co-operation. This element is also illustrated in the story of David and Roger, particularly in the case of Roger, who came to the meeting in order to insure David's not cutting in on his business. This force of competition can be used in working with various organizations. After a start has been made, an appeal can be directed to the various organizations by pointing out that some of their competitors are now within the People's Organization and that as the People's Organization develops in strength this strength and power will naturally be shared by the member organizations. So the member organizations will get stronger and become leaders in the community to the detriment of those who are neither affiliated with nor part of the People's Organization. One organizer described this point thus:

"One neighborhood that I was working in was pretty heavily Catholic and it may surprise you to know that a lot of those churches hated each other's guts. Sure, they were all Catholic churches but there are different kinds of Catholic churches. Now I don't mean that they weren't all Roman Catholic. I mean some were Polish Catholic, some were Slovenian Catholic. Some were Lithuanian, some were

German, others were Slovak, Mexican and a couple of others, including what they call All-Nationalities Church. All-Nationality Churches are also All-American Churches. By that they mean that Catholics of any kind, whether they be German, Polish, Lithuanian, can all come to this church. Now, all these churches were in competition with each other, and I mean it when I say that they really hated each other. It was pretty funny too, because a lot of these priests would get up on Sunday and would give long sermons on the brotherhood of man and therefore love thy fellow man, etc., and the next thing you know they would be walking down the street, bump into the priest from the other church, and cut him cold. When you talked with them they had nothing but scorn for a lot of their fellow priests. Now, in this organization the churches all came together, most of them because they were genuinely interested in doing something about working with the people for a better life. But two of the churches were just staying out until we let them know, and they could see for themselves, that the organization was going ahead and it meant that the competition would get stronger than they were. So they joined up. Now that's all in the past, because today those two churches are actually in it for no other reason except real altruism."

Many people and organizations will originally join a People's Organization simply to use it as a medium for futhering their personal desires for power or money. There will always be a sufficient number of them coming in on that basis so that they will effectively checkmate one another and discover that the only way any of them can make progress is by the entire group's moving forward. In one community it happened this way:

"A lot of our businessmen and a number of our agencies which included a couple of churches joined the organization solely to put a noose around the neck of their competitors. So what happened? We had a lot of groups and people who had nooses around the other guy's neck and it got so that nobody dared to pull his rope any tighter because the other guy might grab his end of the rope and pull too. Of course, one of the jobs in organization is to get all these nooses tied into such a complicated knot that nobody dares to pull his rope.

"In the last analysis all these people and agencies find that they have put their individual objectives into a collective basket and the easiest and best way for them to get what they want is to work with the whole group so that the whole group will get the whole basket. After a while it really isn't such a complicated thing because when these fellows really get to know each other they all forget about the nooses and they stick together because they want to, because they like each other, because they really are concerned about the other guy's welfare *and because they know by that time that the other guy's welfare means their own welfare.*"

A common cause of failure in organizational campaigns is to be found in a lack of real respect for the dignity of the people. Some organizers may feel inwardly superior to the people with whom they are working. An organizer who has this superior attitude cannot, in spite of all his cleverness, all his protestations of belief in the equality of all people, including himself, conceal his true attitude. It repeatedly comes out in a gesture, an expression, or the inflection of his voice. People cannot be constantly fooled. Even when that organizer uses a sympathetic approach, it is a calculated form of sympathy which is apparent to the people.

An organizer who really likes people will instinctively respect them. He will not treat adults as children. He will have the utmost consideration for the

pride and feelings of those whom he is trying to organize. To understand this is to understand the story
of the failures and later success of Muddy Flats.

Muddy Flats lies in the heart of the Bible Belt of
America. Here a number of religious groups, ranging
from a small but strongly organized Catholic church
on the one side through the main arms of the many
Protestant churches—Methodist, Baptist, Seventh-Day
Adventists, Holy Rollers, and fifty-seven other varieties on the other—all flail one another mercilessly,
vengefully, and spitefully with the cudgels of religion.
Each church leads with the Old Testament, and as you
raise your guard, up they counterpunch with the New
Testament. They view a follower of another sectarian
group as being far more depraved than the heathen.

The countryside around Muddy Flats represents
a strange combination of contradictions. During the
Civil War the spirit of secession ranged the streets
side by side with the spirit of Unionism. Southern
and Northern cultural characteristics have fused together into an incomprehensible hybrid. Out of the
country of which Muddy Flats is a part came the flaming, fanatical John Brown. And as John Brown's
body marched on, that part of America took a deep
breath and belched forth Carrie Nation, who
promptly picked up her little axe and declared war on
every saloon in the country. Carrie Nation went the
way of all people and the whole Bible Belt shud-
dered and was convulsed by the intolerance and
cruelty of religious bigotry. Conversion traveled at
the rate of a mile a minute and many Midwestern-
ers were converted and reconverted over and over
again. Religion became the Midwestern measles and
almost everyone caught it. From an adjoining state,
but part of the same Bible Belt, came Earl Browder,
who was the titular head of the Communist party
in America and generally a bitter foe of organized religion. From this same adjoining state came William
A. White with a genuine sense of humor and a real

sympathy for human weaknesses. These people could just as well have come from Muddy Flats, for although the different states are illustrated in different colors in the elementary-school geography books, they are cut out of pretty much the same cloth.

In a valley close by a river sprawled Muddy Flats. Muddy Flats was officially described by the local police chief as "a place where rats, men, women, children, lice, dogs, and pigs exist and die." The people living in Muddy Flats migrated many years ago from the South. Many of them had been share-croppers in Arkansas and many of them had come from the hillbilly villages of Kentucky. None of them had more than a two-room shack. None of them had running cold water, let alone hot water inside the shack. None of them had inside toilets. Not one of them had more than one dollar between him and complete pauperism.

All of them suffered from malnutrition. All of them existed in a state of despair. All of them felt broken, disheartened, and embittered. Most of the parents had watched their children go through typhoid fever and smallpox as if they were ordinary and expected "children's diseases." All of them were grossly exploited and criminally underpaid. All of them suffered through a hell on earth.

Stand in the middle of Muddy Flats holding your nose with your left hand against the fetid odors that always seem to hang over the place like a fog and then, shading your eyes with your right hand from the burning Midwestern sun, look upward and you will see on top of the highest hill what seems to be a page out of a fairy book. You will see beautiful white country homes framed in cool, sweet, green estates. Hanging in the sky like a mirage—a mirage to taunt and drive men to exasperation. But it isn't a mirage, it is the very real site of the homes of the executives and owners of the principal and only industry. The contrast of living is a sin to behold. It represents the

most graphic illustration conceivable of a class structure in society. It would have made a perfect frontis-
piece for *Das Kapital*.

Here in Muddy Flats people went about in their
misery for generations. Here attempt after attempt
had been made by all kinds of groups to organize
these people so that they could literally pull themselves out of this muck by their own bootstraps. All
these attempts had failed.

The reason for the failure of previous organizational campaigns was a simple one, so simple that
it was overlooked by all those who tried to organize
a People's Movement in Muddy Flats. It was a reason also ignored because the individuals who were
trying to organize Muddy Flats really did not like
people to the extent of respecting the dignity of human beings regardless of how they lived. The reason
was that all organizational campaigns contained an
implicit looking down upon the people of Muddy
Flats. This may sound far-fetched but it is actually
the unvarnished truth.

All organizational drives in Muddy Flats emphasized the fact that the people on top of the hill
were primarily responsible for the misery and suffering of the people in Muddy Flats. It so happens that
in this particular case the charge was completely
justified. Organizers coming into Muddy Flats would
say to the people, "Look, don't you understand that
the reason you are suffering in all of this poverty and
disease is because of the way the people on top of
the hill are treating you?" The unanimous response
of the Muddy Flats people was, "Yes." The organizer
would then continue, "We're going to have a meeting next Friday night and we want all you people
there so we can organize to do something about it—
will you be there?" The response was again, "Yes."
When Friday night came around very few, if any, of
the Muddy Flats people were there.

After two or three experiences of that kind, organizers threw up their hands and left Muddy Flats to follow its miserable destiny. They charged that Muddy Flats people were too demoralized, too broken, too crushed ever to be able to stand up and work and fight like human beings. What the organizers would not and did not admit, even to themselves, was that they really did not respect these people; if they had, they would never have thought in those terms.

The reason Muddy Flats people would not show up for the Friday night meeting was that they found themselves in a terrific dilemma. On the one hand they agreed with the organizers that the basis for their condition was to be found in the evil of the people on top of the hill. But then to themselves they thought, "That smart New Yorker must certainly think I'm dumb—I've lived here for forty years in all of this mess and that smart guy has to come around to tell me why I've been living in all this mess. What he's really saying when he tells me that I should come to that Friday night meeting is that I'm too dumb to know the reason for my trouble and that he's smart enough to do something about it. So if I go to the meeting I'm really admitting to him, and certainly to myself, that I am dumb." So he doesn't go.

Then finally an organizational campaign was launched in Muddy Flats with full recognition of this psychological dilemma. It was done in such a way that the people themselves really felt that they had diagnosed their own problems. The organizer, in articulating his own analysis of the problem, did not say, "The trouble with you down here is that the people on top of the hill are exploiting you." He said, "A lot of people in Muddy Flats tell me that to try to understand why things are so tough down here you got to think about the top of that hill up yonder—is that right—what do you think, Joe?" or, "That saying you folks have, 'We feed the cow down here and they milk it up there,' is exactly right. You really put your finger right on the heart of your troubles."

Once the diagnosis of the problem had been made by the local people, the organizer soon found that the people were telling the organizer that the thing to do was to organize: "What about next Friday night for a meeting?" The Friday night meeting was held with 100 per cent attendance. Muddy Flats was organized and Muddy Flats has been doing a good job of cleaning up its problems even though in the hustle and bustle of cleaning an occasional kick or poke of the elbow finds its way up to the top of the hill. Muddy Flats is on its way and the top of the hill will come halfway down to meet it or Muddy Flats will go completely up to the top. Muddy Flats people no longer take typhoid as a "children's disease" and they no longer sit in the darkness of despair. They are alive and fighting. The future isn't bright as yet but one thing they all know—there is a future. There is hope, and life is worth living. There may not be a light at the end of the trail but they have a light in their hands, a light they made themselves, and they know that not only will they themselves have to work out their own destiny but that they themselves *can*.

A significant feature of this approach to Muddy Flats is that in working through (even by suggestion) the local people and their organizations, all proposals carry with them the approval and prestige of these local persons or groups. It is similar to the reaction of an individual to a proposal coming from a stranger as against the same proposal coming from his local minister or priest or any other local person whom he admires as one of his leaders. The approved channels of communication are his own neighborhood or his friends. Anything that he encounters from outside sources is to be critically examined until he determines not only how he feels about it but how the rest of his own people feel about it. It is not important if you disagree with him, but it is almost of life and death importance to him whether his people approve or disapprove. He has to live with them.

The organizer should at all times view individuals or groups in terms of the total social situation of which they are a part. This concept should be so thoroughly understood and accepted and should so completely become a part of the organizer, that he never sees individuals only as individuals or groups only as groups but always sees them as component parts of a total social situation. He knows that individuals and groups must make an adjustment to their social situation because they have to live with it. He knows that the opinions, reactions, and behavior of persons and groups will, to a large extent, be determined by what their own community thinks. Those organizers who fail to understand fully this functional relationship between individual groups and their communities will never survive the first day of an organizational drive. What they will do, and what they have done, is to create a little social situation of their own to which they can adjust—but not the people. The typical conventional community council that we have previously described is a perfect example of that procedure.

Those organizers who fully recognize the relationships between persons, groups, and their community possess an enormously important weapon to use in overcoming obstacles in the building of a People's Organization. Even in those extreme cases where failure crowns the effort of the organizer despite all the tactics, maneuvers, and pressures he has exerted upon the individual, the understanding by the organizer of the significance of the relationship between the individual and the social situation will provide numerous opportunities for eventual success. He knows that in the event of initial failure he must create a new

social situation and induce the individual into it; once
the latter has entered the new situation he must of
necessity adjust to it. This adjustment is the solution
to the original organizational obstacle. A case in point
appears in the following report:

"In an Eastern community I got to be very friendly
with George Sherry, who was one of the most powerful labor leaders in that town. He liked me an aw-
ful lot and he himself was really one swell guy. The
only trouble was that while I was getting everybody
else to join the People's Organization, I couldn't get
George interested. Every time I would see him he
would ask me to have dinner with him and then take
me to a night club where he would indulge in his
passion for strip-tease dancers. Whenever I would
talk about the People's Organization, George would
change the subject.

"After some weeks of this we happened to be at
dinner one night and I propositioned him again on
joining the organization. George got very angry and
raised his voice and shouted, 'Look, Dave, I like you
fine. I think you're grand. Every time I'm with you I
have a swell time, but every time I'm with you, you
get started shooting off your mouth about this People's Organization and I'm telling you this is just a
pain in the neck to me. I am not interested in it and
if you open your yap about it just once more—you
and I are finished—and, Dave, I really mean it!'

"I saw that George really meant it. That night I
wandered around town for I don't know how long.
I kept trying to figure out how I could get him into
the organization. I got back to my hotel after five in
the morning and I still had no answer. Then I suddenly remembered something. I wasn't sure what it
was, but it was sort of a half idea way in the back of
my head about something that had happened to me
or that I had read when I was a kid. That morning I
hurried to the Public Library and pulled out a lot of

the books that I had read when I was a youngster and skimmed through them when suddenly the idea hit me. I knew just what to do. It might not work, but it was the best bet.

"I called up a couple of George's friends who had already joined the People's Organization and were its most enthusiastic supporters and said, 'Look, you want George Sherry to join our organization don't you?' They both responded, 'We sure do, but we've given it up as hopeless.' I said, 'Look, maybe we can work this out. Are you willing to play ball?' They said, 'Sure, what's the angle?' I said, 'It's a simple angle and all I want you to do is this. I am going to call George and ask him to go to the ball game this afternoon along with you two fellows, and myself. I know someone who can arrange box seats for us. Now, all I want you to do is, every time the game gets exciting, like a three-and-two count on the batter or like a guy trying to steal base, you guys turn your backs on the game and start whispering among yourselves. And every time George turns to you and says, "What are you guys whispering about?" why, then you just look a little bit uncomfortable and say, "Well, we're just talking about the People's Organization business, but since we're not supposed to talk it over in front of you we're just talking it over among ourselves."

"'Now you keep that up all through the ball game. Then we four will go out for dinner at the Hotel Hoity Toity and all through dinner you guys get off in these little huddles and again every time George asks you what you are whispering about—give him the same stuff. "We've promised not to talk about the People's Organization in front of you and so we're talking it over by ourselves, and besides that there are some things about this People's Organization that are confidential and since you don't belong we can't tell you about them anyway."

"'After dinner we're going down to the Take 'Em Off Club and see some strip teasers dance and the more the babes take off the busier you guys get in your little private conference. You got it straight?' They said, 'Sure, but do you think it will work?' I said, 'I think so. I'm not sure, but it's worth a gamble.'

"That afternoon we went to the ball game. Every time George would begin to sit down after shouting over a particularly dramatic part of the game he would find his two companions huddled together in one side of the box, busily whispering to each other. In the beginning his reaction was, 'Hey, did you guys miss that catch?' Toward the end of the game it had changed to, 'What the hell is so important to you guys that you miss the best part of the game? What did you come to the game for?'

"By dinner his reaction had changed to, 'What the hell's so important that you have to keep on getting off in corners every ten minutes?' By the time of the strip-tease dance he was saying, 'Look, maybe I can help you out if you'll tell me what's the matter,' and then pleading, 'Since when have you two guys had secrets from your old friend?'

"What we had by this time was a new situation or a new little society which George wasn't part of. The job was to get George into this new situation. The attraction was the fact that first he was being left out of something and secondly that by being left out he was missing important things. Put it another way. George was used to being a leader in his union and in the community, but here we had created another little community and not only was George not the leader, but he was being ignored. He wanted in, and if he got into this new little situation he would have to adjust himself to it. Getting in meant joining up and 'adjustment' meant accepting the program and being part of the organization. The following clipping which, by the way, was on the front page tells the rest of the story:

GEORGE SHERRY JOINS PEOPLE'S ORGANIZATION

George Sherry, prominent labor leader of our city, officially announced the affiliation of his union with the new People's Organization today. Sherry stated, "As the head of —— Union with a membership of 22,000 workers I am happy to publicly announce our affiliation with the People's Organization. It is my considered judgment that everybody should join and get into this fight for a better America. It is a privilege to take my place shoulder to shoulder with those other great leaders in the People's Organization."

Just as the functional relationship between an individual and his social situation can be manipulated to get the individual to join the organization, it can be utilized not only to affect the behavior of individuals but also to change the community situation itself. In the previous case the organizer reported the creation of a new situation and the involvement of an individual within that situation. The case report below presents a more complicated picture, but the basic tactic employed in it is similar to the case of George Sherry. The report of Honest John discloses a clear understanding on the part of the local people of Honest John's social situation, the social situation that his children were living in, and the total social situation of the community which involved both Honest John and his children. The understanding by the local leaders of the functional interrelationship between these situations resulted in an approach which fundamentally affected not only Honest John's own position, the crisis that was imminent in that of his children, but also a serious problem that was concerned with the welfare of the entire community.

"In [one community where a People's Organization was built] the organization found that among the various serious problems confronting them was one which had been a thorn in the side of the community for many years. In this particular area there were a large number of gambling houses. These gambling houses were mainly patronized by people from the outside. The actual presence of gambling was not disturbing to the People's Organization, but what did concern it was that many of the youngsters in the neighborhood ranging in age from fourteen to nineteen years were frequenting these gambling places, placing twenty-five-cent and fifty-cent bets on horses and other games.

"For years the civic social agencies and many reform groups had tried to cope with this problem and for years they had failed. A Delinquency Committee of the People's Organization took up the issue. An officer of the organization made the following report:

" 'We knew something had to be done about our kids going into those gambling joints so we callled a special strategy meeting and looked over the situation. We knew that John Jones owned all the joints and so we took a special look at John Jones. We had the dope on him just like we have it on anybody in the neighborhood. After all, we live here and we get all kinds of information. None of that stuff that comes out of what you call "investigations" but what Mrs. Clancy said to Mrs. Smith over the wash line last Monday. What Jones's best friend said to Pete, the bartender, after he was half stiff. What Jones's wife said to her minister and—you know, the real stuff! We figured out all this and then we got the score on him.'

" 'If we were going to try to do something about the joints, it meant doing something about Honest John Jones. So after we gave Honest John the once-over like I told you, we found out what he wanted out of life. That is one thing you got to know all the time. It's the tip-off. When you know what a guy wants out of life you know how to deal with him. Then you can do good work.'

" 'Well, in looking over Honest John's life we looked at what a lot of people would call the "over-all picture." Honest John had two kids, see, There was a girl thirteen years old and a boy going on eleven. These two kids were the answer. We knew that the one thing Honest John was worried about was what would happen when those two kids got to high school. You know, kids in high school are older and smarter; they know what's going on and they're beginning to get an idea of what life is about. Well, we knew when those kids got to high school that the one thing Honest John was worried about was that for the first time in the lives of his kids other kids would say to them, "Your Pa is a gangster," "Your Pa is a racketeer." The one thing Honest John wanted more than anything else was *respectability*. Besides that, Honest John had made a lot of dough and he had enough to be comfortable for the rest of his life. But what good would all that dough do him if his kids got to be ashamed of him? He needed respectability and needed it bad.'

" 'Now that we knew what Honest John wanted, we were in a spot where we could do some trading. After all, that is democracy, ain't it? Give and take. So we started. We got John interested in the organization. He was sort of hard-boiled about it and figured it was kid stuff and a lot of goody-goody business, but after all we were his neighbors and not a bunch of outside do-gooders and so he began to go around with us and then we began feeding him respectability. He found himself sitting down in neighborhood restaurants with neighborhood ministers, labor leaders, important businessmen, priests, and the kinds of guys that were the respectable leaders. And he liked it!'

" 'A few weeks passed by and then we played our ace. A great big important dinner was being thrown in one of the exclusive clubs in the city. It was for some big famous bigwig who had come to town. Our organization, you know, is pretty big and strong now so the city big shots sent us an invitation to have a couple of representatives down at the party. Well, you can guess the rest of it. We picked Honest John as one of our representatives. He went down to the party and he was seated right next to one of the most famous guys in the country—a personal friend of the President of the United States. His picture was taken with all those big shots around him and he's got it hanging in his parlor now. You couldn't buy that picture from him for love or money.'

" 'The next day we made Honest John chairman of the Delinquency Committee. Je-e-ez, you should have heard the Welfare goody-goodies in town scream their heads off! But we knew what we were doing. So up comes the subject at the committee meeting about keeping the kids out of the gambling joints and Honest John says, "Oh, let's get on to other stuff. I got an idea that all that is going to be straightened out tomorrow." Well, by tomorrow it was all straightened out. Signs went up in every joint that read like this:

EVERY PUNK UNDER THE AGE OF TWENTY-ONE HAD BETTER KEEP HIS PUSS OUT OF THIS PLACE OR HE WILL GET IT FLATTENED
(Signed) *HONEST JOHN*

P.S.—AND I KNOW THE AGE OF EVERY ONE OF YOU PUNKS

" 'And that settled it! That was the end of the problem. But there was another pay-off. Honest John liked respectability so much that he gradually began to close up the joints and began to open up night clubs and today he is one of the best leaders we have in the Organization and now "Honest" John means *"Honest"!"* "

An understanding of the role of the individual in terms of his relationship to the general framework in which he lives brings to light the motivation that underlies his behavior. In order to live in any kind of social arrangement or culture, a person must adjust to that culture. The adjustment process involves the acceptance of traditions, taboos, folkways, mores, values, definitions, and all other social elements which regulate our behavior. The process of adjustment is a continuous series of experiences for the individual in which acceptable and taboo thoughts and modes of behavior are impressed upon him. This social conditioning begins in the earliest days of a person's life and goes on from the time his original environment is limited to his family to the time when his sphere of activities and understanding expands through secondary groups, then the community, and then the general culture of which the community is a part.

The effect of all of these experiences and the social pressures of a person's society leaves its imprint upon the person. This imprint is a combination of all of the factors involved in making a social adjustment. Basically, it involves the person's knowledge of what is right and what is wrong plus the degree of his own acceptance of these social norms. This imprint is known by many different names. Some think of it as morality. Others as conscience. Others as personality. Others as character. Psychologists and psychiatrists call it ego.

Regardless of what name this imprint carries it must be recognized fundamentally as a product of a person's culture. It is obvious that a South Sea cannibal who is brought up to accept completely the eating of his fellow men does not have any qualms of conscience, because the practice is approved by his culture and accepted by him as correct.

Implicit within his character or ego is the person's own private conception of his role in his group and in his community. His own life becomes meaningful only in terms of its relationship to his group and his community. The public status of the person is that which is prescribed for him by his group. Prestige, honor, and power have meaning only in terms of his community. For example, a labor organizer in a community may have prestige within his labor union as a constructive, courageous leader, but on the other hand may be regarded by the business group as a destructive rabble rouser. It is also quite probable that the labor leader's own definition of the part that he plays in the life of the community will not only be different from the conception of the businessmen but even from that of his own union followers.

What is important to us at this point is that the one element common to the ego of all individuals is a private characterization of the place they occupy in the social structure. With few exceptions people like to think they have prestige and recognition in their community. Adolescent daydreams, whether they are of being a movie star, athletic hero, national political leader, or what, do not end with the days of adolescence; they only lessen in intensity. These dreams express the inner yearnings of people who hunger for a place in the sun—preferably a good place. They like to think of themselves as being admired or looked up to by others. In their inner fantasies they are very brave and very great people.

Understanding the personality mechanisms operating within the individual in terms of his status within the group, his private definition of his role, and his inner yearnings that his own definition of his status will some day be agreed to by his group, provides important opportunities that can be utilized in the building of People's Organizations.

This sort of understanding of individual mechanisms was useful in overcoming a difficult organizational problem in an Eastern community, where the organizer realized that no real People's Organization could be developed unless a large church and a very large labor union were brought into it. Both of them working together would provide the foundation for a powerful people's movement, and both were so significant in the life of the area that if either refused to participate in a popular movement it was doomed to failure. To aggravate this situation further, the pastor of the church continuously and publicly attacked the labor union as being communistic, and centered most of his hostility on the union leader whom we will call Mr. Red Rowe. Red Rowe was a Communist by his own admission and he was also looked up to as a fighting, honest labor leader by the people in the industries he had organized. Red Rowe hated the pastor of the church, and privately described him as "a stinking Fascist reactionary," although deeming it not polite to answer the pastor's attacks publicly. Here the organizer reports the tactics used in meeting this issue:

"It was this way: The most important job that had to be done in starting a People's Organization was to get this church and this labor union together. The church and the labor union were the two most powerful organizations in this neighborhood. I asked Red Rowe to come to the first meeting, where we were going to have a few of the local leaders, and I also invited this pastor. Neither one knew the other was coming. I picked up the pastor at his church and took him to the meeting. As we came through the door of the meeting room the pastor saw Red Rowe sitting up in the front seat. He turned to me and hissed, 'There's that Red Rowe, the Communist. No power on earth can make me sit in the same room with that atheist Red!' He walked out. I followed him out, pleading with him to come into the room anyway. He was adamant in his refusal. Finally I took one last gamble. I said, 'Well, I am surprised that you are afraid of him, Pastor.' The pastor turned and roared, 'What do you mean? I'm not afraid of anybody.' I replied, 'Well, all I know, Pastor, is that Red Rowe is still sitting up there and you're running away.' The pastor in a rage shouted, 'I thought I was doing you a favor. You said you wanted to bring the people together and to have them become friends. Now I am going back into that meeting and I am going to denounce Red Rowe as a Communist and that certainly won't fit in with your plans. But you asked for it!'

"With that the pastor hurried back into the meeting room. I realized then that I was really between the devil and the deep blue sea. If the pastor had walked out, his church would not join the organization, and that would mean we could never build a real People's Organization. On the other hand, if he stood up in the meeting and denounced Red Rowe, then Red would walk out, taking his organization with him. Either way a People's Organization could not be built. So far all that had been accomplished was that the pastor was in the meeting room and there was still time left, although it was a matter of minutes to try to work out this crisis. I decided to meet the issue on the basis of ego. The reason for this decision was that the tactic of ego had already worked. That was when the pastor refused to admit that he was afraid of Red Rowe and stormed back into the meeting. After all, very few men will openly admit that they are afraid of anything.

"Red Rowe had just finished addressing the meeting, pledging the full co-operation of the union to the building of a People's Organization, and it was now the pastor's turn to speak. I took the floor and insisted upon the privilege of introducing the pastor. As I remember, I made the following speech: 'You people have watched me since I came into this neighborhood. I think most of you are pretty well satisfied that I have no selfish ax to grind, but don't think I am entirely unselfish. I am selfish enough to insist upon having the honor and privilege of introducing the next speaker. The next speaker is a man whose saintliness is second only to God. If he believed that it was in the best interest of his people to walk hand-in-hand with the devil, regardless of what color the devil was, he would do so. He places the welfare of his people far above any of his personal prejudices or feelings. I give you our beloved pastor.'

"The pastor stood up, looked about him in confusion, and then walked over and shook hands with Red Rowe and gave a speech pledging the co-operation of his organization.

"However, I knew that the effect of this maneuver would not be long-lasting. The next morning I went to see the pastor at his rectory and my apprehensions

were fully corroborated. He greeted me with a frown
and then immediately snarled, 'I don't know what got
into me last night but now that you're here I'm glad
because I want to tell you that—that—vile Red Rowe,
that rotten Communist—' I interrupted, 'Yes, Pastor,
that's why I came over to see you. You know that at
our next meeting certain problems are to be discussed
and on one of these issues Red Rowe wants to know
how you are going to vote.' The pastor muttered,
'Why, that—why should that rotten Communist want
to know how I feel?' I replied, 'I know, Pastor, how
you feel, but, you see, Red Rowe worships the ground
you walk on.' [2]

"The pastor was startled and then looked a bit
sheepish as he said, 'Well, you can tell Mr. Rowe that
I am going to vote this way. . . .'

"I then went over to the union office to see Red
Rowe. After some preliminary remarks I told Red that
I would like to know which way he was going to vote
on a problem that was coming up shortly, because the
pastor was interested in knowing. Red Rowe jumped
out of his chair. 'Why, that filthy Fascist reactionary,
that feeder of religious opium to the masses, why should
he give a damn which way I'm going to vote?' I said,
'Well, I know how you feel about the pastor, Red, but
he thinks you're the salt of the earth.' Red suddenly
looked very uncomfortable. Then he said, 'Well, of

[2] This is probably the most direct appeal to a person's individual ego that can be conceived. The pastor, like any other
person, had a deep and abiding love for himself. We have previously discussed the point that persons also like to have the
admiration and devotion of their fellow men. In this case the
organizer described Red Rowe's attitude toward the pastor as
one which was pretty much the same as the pastor privately
felt toward himself, and certainly wanted other people to feel.
To reject Red Rowe's feelings under these circumstances would
be to reject Red Rowe's definition of the pastor as a person so
great that people "worshiped the ground he walked on." In the
last analysis, to reject Red Rowe was to reject Red Rowe's agreement with the pastor's private definition of his own role—which
is asking much too much of a human being.

course, we all make mistakes and some of us believe everything we hear and I'm sure that there have been a lot of wrong things said about that pastor. You tell him that I am voting this way. . . .'

"Within four weeks from the time of this episode this union leader had placed the entire support of his organization behind the parish's program and the pastor was leading a union organizational drive. Today they smile and laugh about their earlier attitudes. Once they began working together and began to know each other, not only did their actions change but the reasons behind their actions. Today this pastor is one of the most aggressive, informed, altruistic friends of labor, and Red Rowe's opinion of organized religion has undergone a deep change."

Another organizational campaign, which took place in a northwestern community, accomplished equally amazing results by fully appreciating the significance of the individual's ego. Here a People's Organization was rapidly taking shape and presented every evidence of stability and growth, but the organizer was encountering difficulty with a local political official, who had a considerable following within the community, had refused all overtures on the part of the People's Organization for one reason or another, all of which boiled down to one statement: "I've got to have time to think this over."

When the organizer would respond, "Yes, Jim, but it has been four months since I've started talking to you about this," Big Jim's answer would be, "I know, I know, but I have to have time to think this over." The organizer finally resorted to these tactics:

"It got so that this continuous stall by Big Jim was really hurting our chances of getting the organization going. Finally I decided to let logic go to hell and try to work on Big Jim's pride. I had just gone into that town on a visit about two days before so I called Big Jim and asked him to have lunch with me the next day, and to meet me in the hotel lobby. He agreed.

The next morning I wrote a letter to a very prominent person and in the letter I said:

" 'This is to let you know that the People's Organization movement in Ipswich Falls is not getting along too well. The main reason for its present limping along is that one of the most powerful leaders in this town, a man by the name of Big Jim, has not joined the organization. Big Jim has a tremendous following in Ipswich Falls. He deserves that following because he is a man not only of great integrity but of the utmost prudence. Even though he has not been able to make up his mind about joining our People's Organization and even though the fact that he hasn't done so is hurting our organization, I cannot help having the greatest respect for him. I think that this delay is another example of Big Jim's intelligence and prudence. I realize the responsibilities that he carries and what his actions mean to his fellow men, and he wants to know everything about the organization before he makes the slightest commitment. I know that Big Jim is carefully investigating the whole idea of this People's Organization and as soon as he is satisfied and sure of the motives and purposes behind all of this work he will not only join but will be one of the staunchest leaders of the movement. Regardless of what happens here in Ipswich Falls, it will always be one of the finest experiences of my life to have been able to meet a person so fine, calm, and prudent as Big Jim.'

"I put the letter in the envelope and addressed and stamped it and left it *unsealed*. On the outside I scrawled a big PERSONAL. A few moments later Big Jim called from the lobby to announce his arrival. I went down in the elevator and as I came into the lobby I saw Big Jim standing about twenty feet away from the elevator doors. I promptly feigned a bad limp. Big Jim inquired about the limp and I told him that I had slipped in the shower that morning and had hurt my leg and suggested that since it was inconvenient to walk around, we have lunch in the hotel Coffee Shop. Big Jim promptly agreed, and as we began to walk toward the Coffee Shop I snapped my fingers, saying: 'Damn it, there's a letter in my room that I wanted to mail. Excuse me while I go back and get it.' Big Jim said, 'Look, why should you have to go all the way back to your room with that bad limp of yours. Let me have your key and I'll get it.' I said, 'Thanks,' and gave him the key. Big Jim walked to the elevator, and as the doors slammed shut I said to myself, 'Well, maybe it will work.' I was banking on one thing and that is the age-old desire of all people to read other people's mail—and what could make this desire more acute than having the mail marked 'personal.' Big Jim came back in a few moments, and I saw that it had worked. The envelope was now *sealed* and I dropped it into the chute. Then I wondered whether the main part of this tactic had worked—the approach to his pride, or what this organizer I had been talking with called ego. It sure did! We no sooner sat down for lunch when Big Jim said, 'Look, you know I am a very careful man. Some people say that I am what's called a prudent person and I have to be very careful because there's a lot of people who take my judgment very seriously and that's the reason I have been slow in making up my mind about this here People's Organization. But I want you to know that I have checked into it and am joining it right now.'

"One year later Big Jim was the president of the People's Organization and today is one of the staunchest fighting champions for the rights of the common folk."

The recognition and understanding by the organizer of the tremendous significance of *personal identification* is fundamental to the building of People's Organizations. Personal identification is the crux and heart of the People's Organization and will be discussed at greater length later, but we are concerned here with its importance in organizational work. The principle of personal identification, when used consciously and deliberately, provides an enormously important setting wherein the organizer can create and project an infinite variety of tactics. The following report was illustrative:

"The organization had made a lot of headway and from the point of view of its leaders every important part of the community life had been brought into the organization excepting one big business which was owned and operated by Old Man Jones. Old Man Jones was known by that name only to those people in the neighborhood who felt that regardless of how bad anyone was 'we ought to be Christian and tolerant in our outlook.' To everyone else in the neighborhood he was called 'that lousy blankety blankety slimy hypocrite called Jones.'

"I hadn't spent my first hour in the neighborhood before I was told about Old Man Jones. His name was the worst epithet a person could use in insulting an enemy. If you really hated anyone you would describe him as being so foul that he was *almost* as bad as Old Man Jones. Jones was in his middle sixties, a silent, sour-faced person who, if he had one friend, it was a well-kept secret. He was a bachelor, and this fact was always mentioned with the accompanying statement that 'Old Man Jones was descended from a long line of bachelors.' Jones was the kind of person who would make a reactionary look like the reddest of radicals. He had not voted since the days of Calvin Coolidge because of his conviction that both the Republican and Democratic Presidential candidates were much too radical and 'dangerous.' Even the children, in their annual Christmas presentation of Dickens' *Christmas Carol* would muff their lines and refer to Scrooge as 'Old Man Jones.'

"However, Old Man Jones was important in the community in that his business interests represented a significant part of the economic structure of that area. By dint of considerable and persistent work I finally convinced Old Man Jones that he should join the People's Organization. It is true that Jones's reasons were not of the best and were purely self-protection. I remember Jones's looking at me and saying, 'Well, I think things have come to a pretty pass when a man has to get into these things just to make sure that he can keep half his money if the common scum ever take over the country.' I felt that considerable progress had been made in getting Old Man Jones to agree to come along halfway with the organization.

"I hurried to the officers of the organization to inform them that Old Man Jones 'had finally given up and was joining.' My announcement of Jones's capitulation to the organization's officials was greeted by an ominous silence. Finally one of the main officers, who was a prominent labor leader, rose from his chair, leaned against the table, and shouted, 'None of us—and I mean not a single decent person in this neighborhood —would even think of letting Old Man Jones join our organization. We don't have to try to explain why we feel as we do—it's very simple—Old Man Jones was born a bastard, he is one today, and when he dies he will be one. And we're not going to stand for any lousy bastard in our organization. You can't show me one decent thing he ever did in the whole damn world.'

"As soon as this officer finished talking everybody jumped up in such vehement agreement that all I could say was, 'All right, all right, forget it.'

"From the point of view of building a really solid organization, Old Man Jones, however, could not be 'forgotten.' I kept trying to figure out some way of breaking through this deep prejudice against Jones. Finally the idea came. It was born of the belligerent blast of the labor leader who said, 'Old Man Jones was born a bastard.' This remark, plus all of the organizational experience of the past which had emphasized one thing, 'When people get to know each other as human beings they get along,' really gave me the clue.

"About a week later I put the idea into action. During a mass meeting of the People's Organization I was showing pictures of another People's Organization in a different part of the country. These pictures dealt with conditions before the building of a People's Organization and how these conditions had been changed. In the midst of showing these pictures I slipped in a slide picture of a little baby. The audience's reaction was to be expected. 'Ah's' and 'Oh's' were heard throughout the auditorium intermingled with chuckles and remarks of 'Isn't it cute!' 'What a darling baby!' In the midst of this reaction I calmly announced that this was a picture of Old Man Jones when he was a baby! As far as I was concerned I wasn't telling a lie because all baby pictures look pretty much the same and I also knew that at some time in the past Mr. Jones had been a little gurgling baby.

"The audience was silent but the gamble worked. Nobody could look at the picture of that cute little baby and say, 'Old Man Jones was born a bastard.' It hammered across the simple point that Old Man Jones was a human being and at one time he had been a little baby just like they had been or just like their own little babies. It cracked the complete set of attitudes which regarded Mr. Jones as being an inhuman species out of the inferno. It was the opening wedge for a series of other organizational tactics which in a short time ended up with Mr. Jones being accepted into the People's Organization."

The organizer should constantly bear in mind that personal identification manifests itself in many indirect forms. He should be particularly aware of this fact when making his initial organizing talk to a new group, regardless of whether it be a service, fraternal, nationality, racial, political, or labor organization. Frequently he will find that after presenting the purposes of the People's Organization and using every argument at his command to interest this new group in joining, there will always be a certain amount of vociferous and violent objection to both the proposed People's Organization and the arguments advanced by the organizer. The organizer who forgets the significance of personal identification will attempt to answer all objections on the basis of logic and merit. With few exceptions this is a futile procedure. The reason it is useless and the reason the organizer will fail in successfully coping with this opposition is that he fails to consider the system of relationships and personal identifications that are common in all groups.

Whenever an organizer is invited by the officers of an organization to talk to that group he should never forget that all groups have factions; sitting out in the audience is a person who was defeated for the presidency of that organization by the present incumbent —the one who invited the organizer to be present. The same situation holds for all of the other officers of that organization. It is in the best of American traditions that a candidate defeated for office throw his full support behind the victor, but it is in the truest of human traditions that the loser will retain a certain bitterness and frustration from his defeat which he will indirectly express whenever the opportunity presents itself.

The organizer thinks of himself as a guest speaker but he presents a far different image to the defeated candidate sitting in the audience. He has been invited by the incumbent officials and is identified with them; therefore he presents a perfect target for attack by the other faction. By attacking the organizer's position they are really attacking the administration which, by inviting the organizer to speak, has indicated at least a partial approval. At the same time the opposition is maintaining the American tradition of the good loser, since the attack is not aimed at the officials themselves.

The organizer who is conscious of being identified

with the regime that invited him will do one of two things. Either he will in his opening remarks disassociate himself from them, or he will make no attempt to answer the opposition by logic but will wait until the formal meeting is over, then establish a personal relationship with the opposition and assure them that they are as important to him as are the officers of the organization. He will convince them that he is not tied up with any clique, including the present administration.

The latter course is recommended over the first alternative because the public disassociation from those who have invited you is a very delicate process and must be handled with extraordinary subtlety. The slightest bungle and the organizer may find himself in the position of having so successfully disassociated himself from the officers who invited him that he has actually lost their support. If this situation ever develops, the organizer will be in an impossible position. The gravity of this condition cannot be overestimated because even the opposition hates a traitor, and to be invited in by the administration and then openly to repudiate any relationship with them is to commit an action wholly unforgivable by both sides.

A realistic appraisal and definition of these types of tactics came out of an interview between an organizer and one of the most ruthless political machine bosses in the country. The political chief had publicly retired from machine politics because of his advanced age, but behind the scenes he still held the important reins of control. The organizer who entered his dictatorially dominated city found it almost impossible to proceed without at least a neutral attitude on the part of the boss. Local residents were fearful of speedy and drastic political retribution if they incurred the disfavor of the machine. All efforts of the organizer were parried by the people with the question, "How does Old Uncle Bill feel about this?"

Finally, in desperation, the organizer went to see

Old Uncle Bill. The purpose of the visit was not to secure co-operation but simply to get permission
(strange as it may seem in an American city) to
carry on this kind of work. The organizer knew that
once the People's Organization was started nothing
could stop it, but the immediate necessity was to make
arrangements which would allow it to get started. The
organizer's one reason for hope was that Uncle Bill was
so old and had accumulated so much power and prestige that he had reached the point in life where he
could afford to be honest and altruistic.

After being ushered into Uncle Bill's office and introduced to him, the organizer began to explain both
his objectives and tactics. Throughout the next hour
and a half he never once got a frontal view of Old
Uncle Bill's face. The political chief had turned his
swivel chair so that he sat sideways, staring at a blank
wall. What the organizer had hoped would be an interview turned into a complete monologue. Throughout, Old Uncle Bill not only kept staring at the wall
but never changed his facial expression or even gave
the faintest sign of approval or disapproval.

Finally the organizer stopped talking. Uncle Bill
spoke for the first time. Wheeling around in his chair,
he said, "Go on, young man, go on." The organizer got
up. "There's nothing more to tell you. I've shot
my wad." Old Uncle Bill leaned back, stroking his
chin, and then, suddenly looking up, said, "There was
another young feller that came to this town about
thirty or more years ago. He tried to sell me just about
the same bill of goods that you're giving me. His name
was—let me see—it was—oh, yes, a feller by the name
of Lincoln Steffens. I turned him down, but I'm going
to play ball with you and I'll tell you why. This feller,
Lincoln Steffens, figured that every man was real
good and all you had to do was to give him a chance
to be better and by Jiminy, he would get better. But
you"—Old Uncle Bill chuckled—"you, young man,
you believe every man and woman has got a little bit

of larceny in their hearts and you're using that larceny to make them better in spite of themselves and you're damn right! Go ahead!"

Another very different type of tactic, also of wide significance, was being utilized in various parts of the country where People's Organizations were coming into existence. These organizations referred to the tactic as a program ballot. This program ballot consists of one sheet of paper with one printed paragraph at the top of the sheet. The paragraph reads: "If I had my way, this is what I would do to make my city the happiest, healthiest, prettiest, and most prosperous place in the world."

This paragraph is followed by about fifteen blank lines with a space on the bottom for name and address.

In the communities where they were used, these ballots were circulated through every known medium of distribution. They were attached to each of the local community papers, distributed in the churches, the unions, the fraternal, nationality, and all other agencies and groups. They were distributed in the movie theatres, at meetings, and house to house. They provided in the beginning a direct approach toward getting a statement of objectives from the people themselves. The tremendous significance of this procedure was to be found not in its original purpose but in its functioning as an organizational criterion and secondly as an organizational instrument.

Its use as a criterion was graphically revealed in these communities. Only a small percentage of the first distribution of organizational ballots was returned, with conventional needs of the community listed dispassionately. These ballots covered briefly the most superficial issues, such as cleaning up the alleys, increasing the size of the ball field so that a skating rink could be installed during the winter months, repairing the heating in the dressing house of the skating rink, and other issues commonly discussed in the local press and sermons. On the whole it would seem that these were problems that anyone, including any outsider, could think up, representing the people's program.

The same ballots were distributed a year later. This time the response was as different as day is from night. A much larger percentage of the ballots was returned. Instead of brief, dispassionate, conventional writing, both sides of the ballot were covered with writing and in some cases the individual had attached two or three additional written sheets. The written observations were made with emotion and force, and demanded that immediate action be taken. The issues described were deep and fundamental.

The contrast was so great that many of the community leaders felt that these ballots represented proof of another significant point, which is that the local people had been sunk in apathy and nonparticipation over so long a period of time that they had actually forgotten the use of their tongues. They had become inarticulate and almost robot-like in their responses. Through the organizational work of the year they found their tongues and began to think for themselves, and hence the change in both the temper and target of their attacks. This ballot program has become one of the most significant measuring sticks of rank-and-file participation known to these organizers.

As mentioned before, the program ballot was used as an organizational device. First, it made a lot of people aware of the fact that a People's Organization had begun; second, it made them aware of it under favorable conditions—this was one of the rare opportunities where they themselves could help in writing out the program of an organization; third, those who showed sufficient interest to sign their names and addresses were identified to the organizer so that they could be approached personally and brought into the organization; fourth, it gave the administration of the organization an iron-clad defense during the first year against various opposition groups that attacked it by charging, "This organization says that its program represents what we all want. Well, I say that isn't true. How many of you had the chance to sit down and work out this program?" The organization could and did successfully counter this charge with: "This first program came out of the ballots that were put out in the community. It includes everything in those ballots. Everybody had a chance to say what he wanted to be included in the program and if you didn't it was because you just didn't care or you were too busy to help make up the program. But you had the opportunity."

The maneuvers and tactics described in this chapter have been employed solely for the objective of building a People's Organization. They can be utilized only to a limited extent by those whose main interest is manipulation either for the sake of manipulation or for undemocratic objectives. In the last analysis the use of these tactics for evil or selfish purposes will defeat the tactician's own objectives. Underlying all of them is a fundamental approach which so transcends in importance the hitherto described tactics that they are reduced almost to the position of being ornamental. This fundamental tactic is the organizer's own complete faith in people and his complete devotion to that faith.

People know you for what you really are and to think otherwise is to believe that people are fools. They know your inner yearnings and inner beliefs. They know that the organizer's belief in people is the keel of his convictions. His keel must be so deep and so strong that regardless of his different tacks, his course and objectives are clear. Selfish, evil, and small people do not have a keel of convictions and therefore are unable to sail a set course. To those kinds of people maneuvering becomes opportunistic conniving for no other purpose than personal self-satisfaction. They cannot tack against the wind because they have no keel. They are at the mercy of the elements and nothing is more merciless than an outraged people striking at its exploiters.

Those who build People's Organizations can maneuver hither and yon and utilize many of the tactics discussed in this chapter and many of the people will later know of the use of these tactics, but throughout this period the people will not lose their faith or belief in the organizer, because they know that he is doing this or that because of his fundamental belief in them —the people themselves. Their mutual goal is so good and so bright that it is not important if one must go through a few devious valleys and shadows in the struggle for the people's world.

8

Conflict Tactics

A PEOPLE'S ORGANIZATION is a conflict group. This must be openly and fully recognized. Its sole reason for coming into being is to wage war against all evils which cause suffering and unhappiness. A People's Organization is the banding together of large numbers of men and women to fight for those rights which insure a decent way of life. Most of this constant conflict will take place in orderly and conventionally approved legal procedures—but in all fights there come times when "the law spoke too softly to be heard in such a noise of war."

The building of a People's Organization is the building of a new power group. The creation of any new power group automatically becomes an intrusion and a threat to the existing power arrangements. It carries with it the menacing implication of displacement and disorganization of the status quo.

Agnes E. Meyer of the *Washington Post* pointed this out in a study of a People's Organization in Chicago:

These serious-minded inhabitants of Packingtown have never picked a fight, nor have they avoided one when great issues and principles were involved. They have fought because in a competitive city like Chicago, any new power group has to go through battles if it is going to survive. Their thinking on pressure is very simple.

"We believe that democracy is a government constantly responding to the pressure of its people," a group of council members said to me. "The biggest hope for democracy is that Americans will overcome their lethargy and that more and more people and groups will become articulate and formulate their needs." [1]

A People's Organization is not a philanthropic plaything or a social service's ameliorative gesture. It is a deep, hard-driving force, striking and cutting at the very roots of all the evils which beset the people. It recognizes the existence of the vicious circle in which most human beings are caught, and strives viciously to break this circle. It thinks and acts in terms of social surgery and not cosmetic cover-ups. This is one of the reasons why a People's Organization will find that it has to fight its way along every foot of the road toward its destination—a people's world.

Because the character of a People's Organization is such that it will frequently involve itself in conflict, and since most attempts at the building of People's Organizations have been broken by the attacks of an opposition which knows no rules of fair play or so-called ethics, it is imperative that the organizers and leaders of a People's Organization not only understand the necessity for and the nature and purpose of conflict tactics, but become familiar with and skillful in the use of such tactics.

A People's Organization is dedicated to an eternal war. It is a war against poverty, misery, delinquency, disease, injustice, hopelessness, despair, and unhappiness. They are basically the same issues for which nations have gone to war in almost every generation.

A war is not an intellectual debate, and in the war against social evils there are no rules of fair play. In this sense all wars are the same. Rules of fair play are regulations upon which both sides are in mutual agreement. When you have war, it means that neither side can agree on anything. The minimum agreements of

[1] "Orderly Revolution," *Washington Post*, June 4, 1945.

decency that either side may display stem not from
decency but from fear. Prisoners are treated according
to certain minimum standards and both sides hesitate
to use certain inhuman weapons simply because of
fear of reprisal.

In our war against the social menaces of mankind
there can be no compromise. It is life or death. Failing
to understand this, many well-meaning liberals look
askance and with horror at the nakedness with which
a People's Organization will attack or counterattack
in its battles. Liberals will settle for a "moral" victory;
radicals fight for victory. These liberals cannot and
never will be able to understand the feelings of
the rank-and-file people fighting in their own People's
Organization any more than one who has never gone
through combat action can fully grasp what combat
means. The fights for decent housing, economic security, health programs, and for many of those other social issues for which liberals profess their sympathy
and support, are to the liberals simply intellectual af-
finities. They would like to see better housing, health,
and economic security, but *they* are not *living* in the
rotten houses; it is not *their* children who are sick; it is
not *they* who are working with the specter of unemployment hanging over their heads; they are not fighting their *own* fight.

It is very well for bystanders to relax in luxurious
security and wax critical of the tactics and weapons
used by a People's Organization whose people are
fighting for their own children, their own homes, their
own jobs, and their own lives. It is very well under
those circumstances for liberals who have the time
to engage in leisurely democratic discussions to quib-
ble about the semantics of a limited resolution, to look
with horror on the split-second decisions, rough-and-
ready, up-and-down and sideways swinging and cudg-
eling of a People's Organization. Unfortunately conditions are not always such that a board of directors
can leisurely discuss a problem, refer it to a commit-

tee, and carry through with all of Robert's Rules of Order. That luxury is denied to the people who suddenly find themselves subjected to a lightning attack, of what liberals would call a foul character, by the opposition. The people in a People's Organization cannot afford simply to stew in righteous feelings of indignation. They are in a fight for everything that makes life meaningful—and attack by the enemy calls for counterattack.

The People's Organization does not live comfortably and serenely in an ivory tower where it not only can discuss controversial issues but actually possesses the choice of whether or not to take a hand in the controversy. In actual life, conflict, like so many other things that happen to us, does not concern itself too much with our own preferences of the moment any more than it does with our judgment as to whether or not it is time to fight.

A People's Organization lives in a world of hard reality. It lives in the midst of smashing forces, clashing struggles, sweeping cross-currents, ripping passions, conflict, confusion, seeming chaos, the hot and the cold, the squalor and the drama, which people prosaically refer to as life and students describe as "society."

The difference between the conventional liberal protest and the life-and-death type of tactics used by a People's Organization is illustrated by an account of a struggle of one of the most powerful People's Organizations in the nation. One of the leaders of this organization described the methods used in what he called "the battle of the People versus the Tycoons":

"The giant of the retail business life of the Across the Tracks neighborhood is Tycoon's Department Store. Its size, volume of business, and capital indelibly stamp it as 'big business.' Tycoon's stands at the corner of Main Street and Washington Road, in the heart of Across the Tracks. Since the turn of the century it has been standing there, a mountain of glittering merchandise in a valley of misery.

"The size of Tycoon's reflected inversely its interest in the local people. It was the biggest and its financial backing the richest and its prices the lowest. Such a commercial combination seemed impregnable; to hell with public relations. As long as Joe Dokes could buy cigarettes 20 per cent cheaper at Tycoon's he would keep coming regardless of what anyone said. Money talks, and here it was hollering cigarettes $1.30 a carton every place, but at Tycoon's $1.05. Black and White Scotch $3.25 any place, $2.25 at Tycoon's. Why worry about public relations? You got 'em. Money talks. Let the little squirts—the two-by-four stores—do the back-patting of the neighborhood priests or the leaders of church or fraternal organizations, or shell out in contributions for dance programs for youth clubs, or for building a recreation hall in a parish. Let those small businessmen pay off. Suckers! Well, they weren't any better than the people. But not Tycoon's. They were big enough not to have to worry about what this church or that organization thought. They were so big they couldn't see the small people.

"The Tycoon Store completely ignored the local institutions—they never gave any contributions to any of the churches or any other neighborhood organizations—they never showed any interest in the welfare of the community—and their imperious and domineering manner resulted in at least two of the churches asking their parishioners to boycott Tycoon's. Tycoon's met these boycotts with their sure-fire formula—by advertising drastically reduced prices for certain nationally advertised items. Most of the people ignored the advice of their ministers and priests, and business boomed at Tycoon's. There has also been constant complaining and criticism regarding the wages paid by Tycoon's and also the conditions under which employees work. Although Tycoon's cut-priced each local church boycott into failure, they also cut deeper and deeper into the pride and respect of the ministers and priests. Bitterness and animosity began to mount.

"The Tycoon public-relations policy at Christmas probably caused more bitterness than any other single act. For years it had been traditional for Across the Tracks to raise a general Christmas fund in order to provide Christmas baskets for the needy families of the neighborhood. Toward this collection the schoolchildren contributed pennies. But each Christmas this Gulliver-like tremendous department store, which far overshadowed all of the other Lilliputian business houses in the neighborhood, would contribute $3.50 worth of hard candy to the entire fund! According to whispers in the community, the wholesale price of the candy to Tycoon's was approximately forty cents. This action on the part of the Tycoon store infuriated the people of the neighborhood and within two years a slogan sprang up in the community: 'Christmas is coming. Maybe big-hearted Tycoon's will contribute fifty cents' worth of candy instead of forty cents.'

"The icy indifference of Tycoon's made the people boil. Like a snowball getting ever bigger as it rolls downhill so did public anger mount higher and higher. Each passing day aggravated the situation. Each passing week found more and more people articulating what had now become a hatred as cold as the icy indifference of Tycoon's.

"The Tycoon situation had become a tinderbox and the slightest spark would set off a public conflagration. It was also apparent that the Christmas season would be the one time of the year when even the tiniest spark would start the fire.

"In mid-November, 1941, the spark came. Some 250 of the local neighborhood boys who were working at Tycoon's joined a labor union and went on strike. These boys, whom we knew as human beings—many of them we knew by their first names—some of them had been married in our churches—some of them baptized—almost all of them members in the various athletic organizations in our community—these boys were our boys!

"Public feeling against Tycoon's steadily climbed to the explosive point. People in the streets were talking. The slogan of the striking union, 'Life begins at $14 a week at Tycoon's,' began to crystallize all of the latent hatred, prejudices, and antagonism of the local residents against Tycoon's.

"Through the People's Organization the people began to act. A soup kitchen was set up for the strikers. Ministers and priests crusaded their cause from the altars, and organization leaders spoke before their members. An organized people were moving. Plans were drawn up for an all-community strike against Tycoon's. By the last of November it seemed certain that the United States would be confronted with the first 'all-community,' 'all-consumer' strike in its history. An aroused people in Across the Tracks had reached the decision that there should be a complete boycott of Tycoon's Department Store. A community strike with an all-community picket line: ministers, priests, labor leaders, heads of fraternal, social, nationality, religious, business and patriotic societies side by side—120,000 people versus $10,000,000. A battle that could have only one outcome—victory for the people.

"Faced with a battle of these dimensions the People's Organization appointed a War Cabinet to lead them through the Tycoon war. I was elected chairman.

"At the outset I attempted in every possible way to delay any community action. I did this because on the surface there was a jurisdictional dispute involved here in which another union (which, judging from all their actions, had a good solid streak of racketeering in them) had been brought into the picture by Tycoon's and Tycoon's was attempting to hide under the guise of a jurisdictional dispute. They were holding up their hands and saying, 'We're for labor. We just want to know whom to deal with. This isn't a fight with Tycoon's. This is a fight between two unions.'

"If, in spite of all we could do, the situation became such that the People's Organization would be engaged in an action such as a community strike, then it was imperative that such action take place on issues that would be impeccably clean. As it was, we recognized the danger of being maneuvered by Tycoon's into a position where instead of the fight being between Tycoon's and the People's Organization, it would be a conflict between the People's Organization and one of the contending unions.

"Among the many other reasons which, to my thinking, argued for delay was this: In order to make an all-community strike effective against Tycoon's, it would mean not only the removal of all restraints but actually further inciting an already enraged people. While there was no doubt that this could be done and done within twenty-four hours, we had grave concern as to whether a community, once so completely aroused, could be held under control and not engage in acts of violence which would result in discredit to the People's Organization.

"For example, from Tycoon's operations (as will be described later on) certain threats were made against two of our priests and one of our ministers. Once these would get out, John would tell Pete that Father Smith had been threatened. Pete would tell Jack that Father Smith had been slugged. Jack would tell Ted that Father Smith was in the hospital with a skull fracture. Ted would tell Jim that Father Smith was dying and Jim might very well physically assault the Tycoon officials. That's the way stories go and there's nothing you can do about it.

"With all this in mind, we began to stall. Fundamental to our stalling was the general idea that time serves to allay human anger and that delay would lessen the possibilities of the contemplated forceful direct action by the community.

"With the tremendous fire, zeal, and passion on the part of the People's Organization flaming up into dangerous proportions, there seemed to be only one way in which to control it and lead it safely through a logical strategic campaign that would bring victory, and that was to appear to be even more bitter and even more vindictive than the others, then say, 'Follow me,' and take them right around the corner into calm waters. Once again, this is something we commonly do in our everyday life. The common effective approach in trying to defend some person against whom your companion is very bitter is not to say, 'You're wrong; he's really a good guy!' The only result of that kind of approach is an argument, the building of a barrier of hostility, of bitterness between your companion and yourself. The intelligent approach is to pick up the cudgels with your companion and beat them in unison as follows: 'There's no question but that you're right. Smith is a louse. I hate him even more than you do. But you'll agree with me that on this one little point Smith has something on his side, and of course you'll agree with me that he has this too.' And you just keep going until Smith isn't such a bad guy after all.

"However, we were in a real dilemma. First, we had to win the fight. Second, we had to win in such a way that there would be no violence and yet the battle would be sufficiently dramatic to serve as an outlet for the stirred-up passions of our people. In other words, we wanted a bloodless victory.

"We decided to weave the campaign strategy about the one big weakness of Tycoon's: their superior high-and-mighty way of dealing with people—and also, since Tycoon's would fight by no rules, we wouldn't either.

"The People's Organization held a meeting on December 15 and demanded action from the War Cabinet. When we announced that the time had come for action, there was great relief on the faces of those present. I could not help but realize what a strain it must have been to them to go along with our previous policy of stalling. They all began to talk at once. 'Oh, boy—now let's get them.' 'Can't understand why you waited this long.' 'Let's go—let's go—come on!'

"We discussed for some time how to set off the opening gun for the war and finally agreed that we would act as a people's court and give Tycoon's a chance to present their side of the case. Then there could be no charge that we fought them without even giving them a hearing. With this agreed we tried to speak to the president of the Tycoon Company, but his secretary coolly informed us that he was in conference. The haughty Tycoons were running true to form. 'If they only keep it up,' we thought to ourselves, 'we'll win.' After failing to contact them by telephone it was agreed to telegraph them with the understanding with Western Union that the wire would be delivered personally to the president of the Tycoon Company. The following wire was sent:

PRESIDENT
TYCOON'S INCORPORATED
MAIN AND WASHINGTON ROAD

FOLLOWING MESSAGE LEFT THIS AFTERNOON WITH SECRETARY TO PRESIDENT OF TYCOON'S: WE ARE CALLING YOU ON BEHALF OF THE PEOPLE'S ORGANIZATION REPRESENTING ALL OF THE CHURCHES, SOCIAL, FRATERNAL, BUSINESS, AND NATIONALITY ORGANIZATIONS IN ACROSS THE TRACKS. WE HAVE BEEN REQUSTED BY OUR PEOPLE TO INQUIRE INTO THE MERITS OF THE CASE OF THE PRESENT STRIKE GOING ON AT YOUR STORE. YOU OR AN ACCREDITED REPRESENTATIVE OF YOUR ORGANIZATION IS REQUESTED TO BE PRESENT AT TWO PM TOMORROW AT THE COMMUNITY HALL OF THE ACROSS THE TRACKS ORGANIZATION. IT HAS BEEN AND AL-

WAYS WILL BE THE POLICY OF THE ACROSS THE TRACKS OR-
GANIZATION TO GIVE A FAIR HEARING TO BOTH SIDES BEFORE
TAKING ACTION.

> WAR CABINET, PEOPLE'S COURT
> ACROSS THE TRACKS ORGANIZATION

"This telegram to Tycoon's president requested him to appear, before a people's court, to defend his company's case against the strikers. We informed them that after the hearing the Across the Tracks Organization would reach a decision and act upon it. Tycoon's indignantly refused to accept the invitation, hysterically charging: 'People's Courts—they have those in Russia! This is the United States of America—we believe in the American law, not in People's Courts.'

"With the absence of Tycoon's president from the hearing, the War Cabinet of the Across the Tracks Organization listened to the case of the union and found in their favor. They then issued a terse statement to Tycoon's asking them if they saw any reason, in view of their verdict, why the Across the Tracks Organization should not take steps to enforce their decision.

"Within an hour Tycoon's attorney was on the phone. He insisted on our coming down to his office. I was prepared to refuse him, but upon glancing out of the window I noticed a driving snowstorm—what a perfect opportunity for a demonstration of the arrogance of Tycoon's in asking that five priests, three ministers, four businessmen, and three labor leaders trudge through the cold wintry snows to meet with a lone Tycoon lawyer! Also, his being a Tycoon lawyer would provide a perfect setting out of which to come in from the cold—we, the humble poor from Across the Tracks coming into an office suite furnished at the cost of thousands of dollars. I accepted the invitation. The plan worked beyond my wildest dreams. We came in out of the snow to the luxurious offices of Van Snoot, Van Snoot, Van Snoot, and Snoot. Snoot made the horrible mistake of attempting to impress us with all his opulence and power. Because there was an insufficient number of chairs in the conference room, he suggested to one of the priests that he pick up one of the chairs out in the hall and carry it in. That was the crowning blow. It was not the specific act itself, but just that it fit into the general picture of the disdain and contempt of Tycoon's and their representatives for the common people.

"During the meeting Mr. Snoot admitted that the majority of the store employees were enrolled in the membership of the striking union but he attempted to portray the dispute as one between the striking union and another union widely suspected of racketeering, with Tycoon's being the innocent victim. Throughout, Mr. Snoot's manner toward us was one of condescension. Our position was simply this: We were not interested in the alleged jurisdictional fight per se. We believe in the law of the land according recognition to the rights of workers to choose their own unions and bargain collectively. If the majority of the employees preferred the striking union, that settled that; and from what Snoot had said it appeared that Tycoon's sided with the racket union and was deliberately fighting the striking union. We charged collusion between Tycoon's and an alleged competing union which by their own admission was nonexistent. Snoot arose in a rage and bellowed: 'Are you people casting insinuations against the integrity of our clients, the Tycoons?' We all laughed. Someone said: 'We're not insinuating; we're saying so.' Snoot sat down, and a grim look came over his face. 'I'd like to have your names and organizations,' he said as he picked up a pencil. 'What for?' we inquired. 'For the record,' he replied. I pressed him: 'What record?' He flushed. 'The record—you know, the record!' 'I don't know,' I answered. Snoot looked very stern. 'Are you afraid of giving me your names?'

"I thought to myself, 'Well, why not? This is a fight for keeps, and as far as what Tycoon's will do with the names—it will probably be some action that will rebound to our advantage—for, judging from their acumen to date, Tycoon's can do no right. We gave him our names and then walked out into the snow-storm.

"The next morning it began. Groups of armed thugs professing to represent the competing union descended upon our neighborhood and threatened those of us who had given our names to Snoot with bodily injury and worse if we did not withdraw from the case. In their dark threats of violence they included and named the ministers and priests. Statements such as these were made to individual members of the Across the Tracks Organization: 'If you want to stay healthy, stop fooling with Tycoon's,' or 'If you want to keep on breathing get your ass out of this fight—and we mean business.' To our questions as to where they got our names they replied, 'You know damn well where we got them.'

"We called Snoot and he admitted turning over our names to this union. We told him what had happened and he calmly replied that he wasn't responsible for their actions. We said, 'You think so—listen, fellow, if you start an automobile, put it in gear and then jump out, you're responsible for what happens. You turned our names in to a bunch of killers and whatever may happen is your responsibility from now on.'

"'Wait a minute—wait a minute—' he broke in. There was stark panic in his voice. We hung up.

"That night we decided the time had come to attack. This was it. The Tycoon blunders had rendered them so vulnerable that a certain line of strategy might well win the war with none of the disastrous effects that we had feared.

"Here was the psychological moment to attack, both to win the war without a war, and yet to provide a satisfactory outlet for the high-running passions and aggressions of our people. With this as our purpose we drew up the following plan of strategy: First we would prepare an attack of such devastating proportions and so utterly diabolic in character that in some respects it would even shock the morals of such people as the Tycoon officials. With the stage thus set, parts of the curtain would be carefully raised in front of Tycoon's stoolpigeons so that the full picture would be conveyed back to the Tycoons, with the underlying understanding that this was just what we were going to do in the preliminary skirmish—God help you once you taste what we will actually do in battle. Our objective was very clear. If we could pulverize the Tycoons with fear and force their capitulation, the victory would be won. In that case the terrible cost of a long struggle would be averted.

"We then began to set up the nightmare props on our stage. First, operating upon the golden rule of 'Do unto the Tycoons as they would do unto you,' we set up the machinery to bait the Tycoons as subscribers to a totalitarian ideology as expressed by their low wages, use of mobsters and gunmen, and general un-Americanism in refusing to acknowledge the rights of organized labor. Following the threats against our officers, among them ministers and priests, which were made on a Saturday, we prepared to go to court on Tuesday and request an injunction restraining Tycoon's, Incorporated, from murdering Protestant ministers and Catholic priests. While we probably would not have been granted an injunction, nevertheless the publicity attendant on our action would have blown the Tycoon empire clear out of business. Tycoon's had presented us with our trump card. This and other Tycoon blunders were turned about to form a horrible Frankenstein's monster.

"The stage was set on Sunday. A Tycoon stoolpigeon was given a peek under the curtain with the announcement of Tuesday as D-Day and ten A.M. as H-Hour. The chips were down and if now Tycoon's did not capitulate it would be a long and bloody war. Monday night the president of Tycoon's, Incorporated, surrendered unconditionally.

"Although this has nothing to do with the fight, what happened after the Tycoons gave up certainly proved our point about all kinds of people being able to work together in a People's Organization once they got to know each other.

"Tycoon's joined the People's Organization and today they are not only among the most popular, respected, and loved members of the community, but one of the chief officials of Tycoon's has been elected and re-elected to one of the most important posts in the People's Organization."

From a People's Organization located in a Western community comes a report on conflict tactics which reveals the hard-headed abilities and pragmatic approach of the rank-and-file citizenry when they are given a chance to fight their own battles.

"Our People's Organization was still sort of in its swaddling clothes, but as an infant we were pretty robust and anybody could see that we were on our way. The Political Machine got a little bit nervous. They watched us for a while and of course we watched them, and pretty soon the blow-off came.

"The scrap really started in the middle of November. The local political henchmen started going around to our merchants, asking for financial contributions to the Political Machine's Christmas-basket fund. You see, the Machine had made a habit of handing out Christmas baskets every year to a few families in each precinct and they could count on that to really work during election time and get out the vote. Well, some of the local merchants came across with ten to twenty-five dollars. The politicians got mad and some of them said to the businessmen, 'Why, you fellows have given the People's Organization as much as a hundred to three hundred dollars apiece and now you're only throwing single and double sawbucks our way—who do you think is running the neighborhood, the Machine or the People's Organization?'

"The businessmen answered that they figured it was the People's Organization—and that was the blow-off!

"The next day it began. Hordes of building inspectors came down into the neighborhood and started going through the stores and telling our businessmen that a wall had to be knocked out of there or a fire escape had to be built over there—you know, the old racket.

"Our businessmen came to us and we knew it meant war. Not really war because what it really was was a big skirmish, but we knew we had to win that skirmish or lose so much face that we would be finished. So we set up a war cabinet and we figured it out this way:

"We were a pretty young organization and we hadn't had a chance to get across any kind of an educational program or ideas among a lot of our people. A lot of them still figured Christmas baskets were a good thing. The people that were in the People's Organization weren't interested in Christmas baskets with just a nice handout in them, but they were interested in what we all wanted—baskets full of jobs, health programs, good housing, and things like that. We figured the only thing we could do would be to speak the language that our people understood. Well, then, if Christmas baskets was the kind of language they understood we would have to speak to them that way until we all learned the real language of the real values: the baskets of jobs, and health programs, and housing that we wanted.

"So we started making a collection among our merchants. Well, you would be surprised how much dough a lot of people have in their sock and how they will pull it out to carry on their *own* fight. Why, one of the churches alone contributed a thousand dollars. Before we knew it we had more money than the Political Machine had; and not only that—our money would reach further because we could get our stuff wholesale through our merchants who were members of the organization.

"The next thing was to get a list of the names of all of the families that the Political Machine was going to deliver Christmas baskets to. We got that list. How, I'm not saying, but in this kind of a fight anything goes. Well, along came Christmas Day and at around ten o'clock Christmas morning a lot of the neighborhood families got the Political Machine's basket with a chicken, pint of whisky, and a couple of doodads. These baskets were given to the families with the compliments of the Political Machine. Around eleven o'clock our boys got around and gave them Christmas baskets that had an eighteen-pound turkey, a quart of whisky, and bigger and better doodads. They got those baskets with the compliments of the People's Organization. If that was the language our people understood, well, we were going to talk it, and talk it right down their alley.

"The next day there was peace and we weren't bothered by the Political Machine for a long time after that. But even though a lot of other fights had been a lot bigger and much tougher, I don't think there was any fight in which the stakes were more important. You see, the biggest problem for a People's Organization is to be able to live through its baby days until it gets big enough to stand on its own feet and trade punch for punch. If ever we could have been knocked out it was at that time, but the Machine made the mistake of just having a skirmish with us instead of smashing us in a war."

Another illustration of conflict tactics is to be found in the following report from a Southwestern community where the People's Organization was opposed by powerful vested economic interests. One of its leaders describes the conflict and its outcome:

"In our town a clique of real estate operators and the railroad practically ran the show. They were known as 'the Combine.' The Combine became more and more fearful of the growth of our People's Organization. Finally they declared war. As in all fights, we used everything we could. We were ready to throw the bucket and the kitchen sink and so were they. Well, we thought it over and decided to capitalize on every bit of our People's Organization. The Combine started the fight by spreading rumors about the People's Organization throughout the neighborhood. The rumors spread like wildfire. Well, our people sat down and we began to talk it over and one of them got up and said, 'There is only one way to fight this, and that is the way we fight forest fires. You build another fire that burns back into the first and that's the end of it.'

"Having decided on the course of action, the officers of the People's Organization looked over their own setup and were attracted by the name of one woman who was an officer of the organization. Her husband headed up a powerfully tough gang in the city. Then our People's Organization went into action. We sent a lot of our boys into various bars and we told them that after two or three drinks they should begin acting pretty plastered and start talking. Their talk was about 'the inside stuff on the People's Organization,' which included whispered insinuations of bribery and corruption of character of the officers of the People's Organization. The story very quickly got into the hands of the henchmen of the Combine and they began giving wholesale distribution to these rumors. In the course of disseminating this story the various local residents who were secretly tied up with the Combine identified themselves. Then suddenly the People's Organization reared up in rage and accused the Combine of besmirching the character of the lady who was one of our officers. Her husband was infuriated and threatened the Combine representatives with dire consequences. While the Combine reeled from the shock of the sudden turn of events we took the offensive and from that time on the fight was pretty much over."

Let us suppose, however, that the People's Organization is in no position to fight on anything like equal terms. A leader of a Western People's Organization makes the following comment on tactics in such a case:

"There is one thing that should always be remembered in case your organization gets jumped on in its early days—the days when it isn't very strong. Of course, if the People's Organization is stronger than the opposition, then the answer is simple: you just crush the opposition. If the opposition is stronger than you, you can first try to equal or surpass their strength by alliance with other groups. But if you cannot do this and the fight begins with the opposition being far stronger than you are, then I would urge the following: First, always remember that when the opposition begins to move in on you not only with greater strength but with a plan that will inevitably result in your defeat—smash the plan! The smashing of the plan of the opposition is nowhere as difficult as people think it is. Every step of this plan is based on an anticipated move from you. Simply speaking, let's take the role of a boxer: he comes in planning to hit you in the stomach so that you will lower your guard, and once your guard is lowered he will hit you in the face. Once he hits you in the face and you raise your guard to protect your face he will hit you in the stomach. Each blow, each move, is based upon a conviction that you will respond in a foreseen manner. Don't respond in that manner and your opponent's plans reach an impasse. Don't react in the conventional, expected manner; don't follow a plan of your own. Go into a state of complete confusion and draw your opponent into the vortex of the same confusion. At least you have a chance that you wouldn't have in a battle of fixed plans and fixed forces where the opposing forces are far superior to yours."

An extremely significant feature of conflict tactics is that practice, used by some organizers and leaders of People's Organizations, which they refer to as "having a fight in the bank." "Having a fight in the bank" has become one of the main principles in some of these People's Organizations. It is based on a realistic and valid psychological appraisal of the functioning of organizations and individuals.

Every so often a disagreement arises between a People's Organization and a small outside agency which is so minor in character that it is a waste of time even to take issue with it. The secretary of the People's Organization will record the disagreement and file it in the record—which is "the bank." As long as the "bank" has a sufficient number of deposits or minor conflicts, the conflict tacticians of the People's Organization are on relatively safe ground with reference to future major conflicts. The thinking underlying this practice is this: the Organization leaders know that when they are involved in major struggles they have to be concerned not only with the issue of victory but also with the manner in which that victory is achieved. They know that when the People's Organization embarks upon an important fight, it means that the rank and file and the smaller leaders of the organizations must be whipped up to a fighting pitch. Some call it morale. From the point of view of straight fighting tactics, the feelings, drives, and aggressions of the people and the organizations that make up the People's Organization constitute the armament of the People's Organization.

Only in rare cases have groups witnessed the fury of an aroused people, and as a result frequently the opposition will capitulate without a fight. Once this occurs the leaders of the People's Organization find themselves in an extremely difficult position. While they have scored the victory, they recognize that some satisfactory outlet must be found which can drain off the aroused aggressions of the People's Organization. They know that unless a satisfactory outlet is found these drives will be turned inward and will express themselves in the breaking out of minor feuds within the organization. As one leader of a People's Organization put it, "Everybody got really hot about the fight and we were all set to fight—then the other side quit. Well, you just can't turn around to people and say, 'Forget everything,' and expect everybody to calm down just like snapping your fingers."

When that situation arises the tactical leaders of a People's Organization will usually request the secretary to review the "fights in the bank" and select one or two which will serve as the outlet. Suddenly some small agency which has been preening itself about having a dispute with the People's Organization and the People's Organization not having done anything about it finds itself subjected to, and completely overwhelmed by, an unexpected attack. All of the "fights in the bank" are legitimate ones. Those small agencies that find themselves attacked months later as a result of the draining-off tactic merit being attacked. An example of the recognition of the importance of this tactic is found in the report of the People versus the Tycoons in which the organizer, after describing the arousing of emotions in this People's Organization, states:

"However, we were in a real dilemma. First, we had to win the fight. Second, we had to win in such a way that there would be no violence and yet the battle would be sufficiently dramatic to serve as an outlet for the stirred-up passions of our people."

The foundation of a People's Organization is the community, and the foundation of conflict tactics is community traditions. Just as knowledge of the terrain is of the utmost importance for military tactics in actual warfare, so too is the knowledge, the full understanding and appreciation of the power of local traditions. The first maxim in conflict tactics to all leaders of People's Organizations is that *the tradition is the terrain.*

We have seen in every actual conflict tactic how organizers and People's Organization leaders have utilized the place or role of traditions and values in the community in maneuvering the opposition into a vulnerable position. The traditions of a community are so strong that a resourceful People's Organization leader can utilize these traditions to defeat opposition which is far stronger and far bigger than the actual People's Organization. In many cases the stronger the opposition is, the deeper and more seriously will it impale itself upon the spearheads of community traditions.

The description of the conflict of the People versus Tycoon's brings this out clearly. The exploiting by the organizer of the demand by Tycoon's attorney that five priests, three ministers, four businessmen, and three labor leaders go downtown to meet him, instead of his going down to the community, fitted in perfectly with the community tradition of resentment against Big Business.

A historical illustration of the role of tradition in conflict was found during the critical days of the French Revolution. The Revolution itself was almost lost because of the inertia and fear of the general populace. Thomas Paine's *Rights of Man* vividly described what the violation of tradition meant to the French Revolution:

The foreign troops began to advance towards the city. The Prince de Lambesc, who commanded a body of German cavalry, approached by the Place of Louis XV, which connects itself with some of the streets. In his march, he insulted and struck an old man with his sword. The French are remarkable for their respect to old age, *and the insolence with which it appeared to be done, uniting with the general fermentation they were in, produced a powerful effect, and a cry* To arms! to arms! *spread itself in a moment over the city.*

The enormous importance of tradition in shaping the life of man is a common and accepted fact. What is not too well recognized is that violation of tradition has from time to time unleashed powers which have drastically altered the course of mankind.

9

Popular Education

In the last analysis the objective for which any democratic movement must strive is the ultimate objective implicit within democracy—*popular education.* Thomas Jefferson's confidence in the eventual realization of the full potentialities of democracy was based on popular education: "Enlighten the people generally, and tyranny and oppression of body and mind will vanish like spirits at the dawn of day."

The very purpose and character of a People's Organization is educational. The bringing together of the many diversified elements of the American population results in the acquisition of knowledge and a consequent changing of attitudes on the part of all of these various elements. Businessmen, labor leaders, religious leaders, heads of nationality, racial, fraternal, and athletic groups all get to know each other. Through constant exchange of views and by sharing common experiences there comes not a so-called "better understanding" between these various groups, but simply *an understanding.* This mutual understanding is accompanied by a new appreciation and definition of social issues.

During hard times the businessmen of the community assume that the problem of unemployment is mainly the burden of business; that when people are unemployed the businessmen have to pay taxes for relief and at the same time suffer from lack of business. There are many labor unions, on the other hand, that feel that unemployment is mainly a burden on labor because unemployed men can't pay dues and are constantly requesting financial aid from the union. The churches feel that unemployment is primarily the heavy cross of the church because when men are unemployed they are wholly concerned with the fundamental job of getting bread for themselves and their families—and in addition there are not only few contributions coming in to support the church but an ever increasing flow of supplications for help from the church.

Through the People's Organization these groups discover that what they considered primarily their individual problem is also the problem of the others, and that furthermore the only hope for solving an issue of such titanic proportions is by pooling all their efforts and strengths. That appreciation and conclusion is an educational process.

More important is the fact that leaders of groups that have seemingly conflicting interests get to know each other as human beings by working together on joint programs of mutual concern. They get to know each other as Johnny and Fred. They learn that they both admire the same ball team. They both cuss when they have a flat tire. They both are filled with the cute sayings of their three- and four-year-olds and essentially they both want just about the same things out of life. Where they differ is in the means to be used in achieving the end.

One of the most common experiences during the early days of a People's Organization is the constant reactions of leaders from various groups along these lines: "Well, Freddy, I had no idea that you guys felt that way about it. Of course, I never knew about how you fellows saw it, but you've certainly got something on your side too." This educational process represents one of the cardinal premises of a People's Organization.

The Organization is convinced that when people get to know one another as human beings instead of as symbols or statistics, a human relationship—carrying with it a full constellation of human attitudes—will inevitably result. It would seem that this point is so patent that it is unnecessary to elaborate, and yet, as with many fundamental precepts, it is so obvious that while we talk about it we completely overlook its significance for practical purposes. A simple illustration is in the reading of the morning paper as part of our breakfast routine. The front page carries a detailed account of the threat of starvation facing millions of people in India. We continue to turn the pages and suddenly our attention is riveted by a small item on page 19 that informs us that one of our friends has been seriously injured in an automobile accident. The emotional impact brings about a sudden cessation of our breakfast enjoyment. Our reaction is one of shock and sorrow. Here is one individual injured in an accident that evokes all of the human sympathy within us. But the millions of Indians have no relationship to us and mean nothing to us. The millions of Indians add up to impersonal digits, but that one friend of ours is not a symbol or a digit, but a warm human being whom we know as a person. We know our friend suffers pain just as we do; in essence, our knowing him as a human being serves as a strong bond of identification. That is the human relationship.

You obviously cannot get everyone in the community to know everyone else on a personal, human basis, but you can get the hundreds of little local leaders to know one another on a human basis. These little local leaders may be shop stewards in their union. They may be active in the P.T.A. They may be officials in their religious organizations. They may be heads of athletic groups. They may be bartenders, precinct captains, or small businessmen. They are the people we referred to earlier in our discussion of native leadership—the "Little Joes." They are the Little Joes that have some thirty or forty followers apiece. Their attitudes significantly shape and determine the attitudes of their followers.

Any labor organizer knows of the Little Joes. When a man is being solicited to join a union he will usually respond along these lines: "Everything you say sounds pretty good, Mister, but before I sign up I want to know if Joe has signed up." If the organizer says he has, the reply will be, "Well, if Joe has signed up, what are we waiting for?" If the organizer says that Joe has not joined, the potential member will answer, "Well, I think you're right, Mister, but I want to think it over and I'll let you know some time tomorrow." The organizer knows full well that the prospect is not going to reach a decision until he talks it over with Little Joe that night. He knows also that Little Joe's decision that night will be the prospect's decision the next day.

These Little Joes are usually totally ignored in all programs superimposed by well-meaning outside agencies, whether they be in the field of reaction or adult education. *But these Little Joes, who are the natural leaders of their people, the biggest blades in the grass roots of American democracy.* These Little Joes present not only the most promising channels for education, but in certain respects the only channels. As the Little Joes get to know one another as human beings, prejudices are broken down and human attitudes are generated in this new relationship. These changes are reflected among their followers, so that the understanding or education begins to affect the attitudes of thousands of people.

The major task in popular education that confronts every People's Organization is the creation of a set of circumstances through which an educational process can function. If we think of education as a high-powered motor car, it is obvious that its use is dependent upon roads. Regardless of the quality of the car and our ability as a driver, the fact remains that unless we have roads on which to travel we can have only limited use out of the car. So it is with education. One may have the finest teachers, the best libraries, the most beautiful buildings, but unless the people have a desire to use these facilities, all the teachers, buildings, and libraries will not advance the cause of education.

A People's Organization is constantly searching and feeling for methods and approaches to make the community climate receptive to learning and education. In most cases the actual procedures used to further popular education will not be independent projects but simply a phase of every single project which the People's Organization undertakes. Here again popular education becomes part of the whole participating process of a People's Organization. The following report from an organizer vividly illustrates how sensitive awareness on the part of a People's Organization can create circumstances that speed the flow of educational programs.

"As you know, our People's Organization is very strong and tied right into the masses of the people living in our neighborhood. We are sufficiently powerful so that educational programs can be spread through the community just about as fast as somebody can crack a whip. You remember when we had reports about some of our children beginning to show signs of rickets? Well, the Executive Committee took it up, came to the decision that one of the reasons for the rickets was that a lot of our children were not getting sufficient vitamins—for instance, the vitamins that are found in orange juice. One reason for this is that many of the folks in our neighborhood are immigrants. They have come from Germany, Poland, Czechoslovakia, Hungary, Italy, Yugoslavia, Lithuania, and a couple of other countries. Lots of them have carried over the habits and diets of the Old World. It wasn't a case of the kids not getting enough to eat, but rather that they were not getting the right kind of food.

"Well, one of our first jobs was to find out whether or not oranges cost more than the kind of food our parents were giving to their children. After all, you can't educate people to give their children orange juice if they can't afford to. That's the big trouble with our whole school system in this country. The kids are all educated to live a kind of life that they may never have a chance to live. A kid in the slums goes to school and is taught all about how to be President of the United States and he's told that's what he should try to be, when the fact is he will be darn lucky if he ever gets to be a truck driver. You know how mixed up our school system is.

"Well, to get back to the main story, we checked on the price of oranges and the price of the kind of food our kids were getting, and we found out that it wouldn't cost our people any more if our kids got orange juice. So we began to educate our people about orange juice. How? Well, the Executive Committee decided on Saturday afternoon that our children had to start getting orange juice in a hurry and they sent the word out through the neighborhood. Here's what happened when the message was received: Every sermon in all of the churches, regardless of denomination, was immediately scrapped and all of the sermons for the next day, or Sunday, were on orange juice. On Monday, when people went to work, they were told by their union stewards that the kids ought to get orange juice. When they sat down for lunch with some of their friends who belonged to nationality societies, it was orange juice. When they got the local paper, the front-page editorial was orange juice! Their wives who had been over at their women's clubs came home saying it was orange juice, and by Tuesday morning one could be reasonably sure that a lot of the children were getting orange juice.

Now, that's a perfect illustration of quick and effective action that can come only from a really strongly united People's Organization. But the trouble is that there are many occasions when this type of approach cannot be used. When you find you can't educate anybody because of circumstances that act just like a brick wall between you and the people you're trying to reach, then you have to make new circumstances.

While you can, for example, talk over with your people life insurance, health problems, housing, or any number of social and personal problems, there are certain subjects that are taboo. One of these is personal finances or *how a person should spend his own money.* On this subject not even a person's priest or minister can even begin to give him *unsolicited* advice. How a person should spend his own money is regarded by that person as his inalienable American right and nobody else's business. To venture into a discussion on this subject with a local person is to insure that you will be told to "mind your own damn business." This subject is one of those islands of privacy into which no outsider can safely intrude uninvited, regardless of his relationship with a person.

Here is a concrete example of the problem: it was noticed that in a certain neighborhood there were a number of people—few, to be sure, but enough to be disturbing—who, although they earned no more than a pittance each week, would nevertheless annually blossom forth with a brand-new car—and always a big one, a Super. It was also known that the children of these same people were not well clothed, their houses were poor, they lacked a refrigerator, they were in debt to a private finance company for an average amount of about $300 on which they paid a minimum of 33⅓ per cent interest—with the result that after paying the interest every year, at the end of the year they still owe $300. They had very little if any life insurance, so that in case of tragedy the family would be left virtually penniless. In short, their entire family life rested upon an economic quicksand.

This insecurity gave rise to irritability, tensions, and finally arguments. It was a deeply rooted cause of family disintegration. The question of course came up as to why these people would purchase a new Super every year. The answer was to be found in the salesmanship and installment-payment character of our present kind of business culture. The important thing is to sell and make a profit, and questions of whether the purchaser is buying to his own disadvantage or whether the purchase will create a grievous condition within his family are not worthy of any consideration.

A careful scrutiny of why Joe Dokes got his annual Super reveals that he was victimized along the following channels: Joe Dokes originally went out to purchase a second-hand car that would cost him around $250. Once he came into the market for a second-hand car he was promptly sold the idea that it was pointless to waste $250 purchasing a second-hand car which would require constant upkeep and would have very little trade-in value for the future, when for a few hundred dollars more he could get a brand-new Poop. Once interested in the Poop, he discovered that the price of additional accessories plus a number of other items, such as bumpers, put the car in a sales class very close to that of the next larger-sized car. One thing led to another, and finally he was sold on getting a very good buy in a Super, because "after all instead of having a Poop you have a Super and it will trade in for more money next year; it is more comfortable, safer, and you don't have to pay for it—all you have to do is sign some papers and pay just a couple of dollars more a month than you would for a Poop." These arguments plus the prestige factor in driving an expensive automobile resulted in Joe Dokes's economic dilemma.

Similar processes would be repeated the following

year. Joe Dokes would drive in the next year not to purchase a new car but simply to get some repairs done. Once again he was caught in the toils. "After all, Mr. Dokes, if you repair your car it still is an old car and every month you can figure on about fifteen dollars worth of repairs—not only that, but next year it will be two years old and your resale value will be so much lower. Now all you have to do is sign those little slips and you don't even have to put any money down. . . ." So Joe Dokes drives home in a new Super.

"Well, there was little we could say to Joe Dokes about it," reads the local organizer's report, "but we gave it a lot of thought. What we had to do was to build a bridge that would go over this valley of 'private affairs' so we could get through to Joe and so we could give him some *education* on finances. With that idea in mind we organized a Credit Union that practically everybody in the neighborhood belonged to —anybody that belonged to a church or union or a fraternity or any agency that was part of the People's Organization automatically was a member of the Credit Union. Well, the next year Joe went down to get his Super, but before he signed up he figured, 'Why should I pay this kind of interest and service charge when I can go down to the People's Organization's Credit Union and borrow the money and pay for the car all at once? I can really save money doing it that way because it will cost me only one per cent at the Credit Union and I won't have to pay any of these here service charges.'

"So Joe comes down to our Credit Union and, brother, we're just laying for him. He doesn't need an investigation because we got his priest, his labor-union leader, the head of his wife's women's club, and people like that on the committee. Joe asks us for five hundred dollars. Our answer is something like this:

"'Joe, we'll give you the five hundred, but *not* for a

car. We will give it to you if you will spend it this way: You take three hundred of it to pay off that loan to the private finance company, so instead of owing them the money at thirty-three and a third per cent or more you will owe it to us at one to three per cent and in that way you will be able to pay it off and get your head out from under water. We'll help you to finance a second-hand refrigerator for about thirty dollars. Until we get all-community life-insurance programs we figure that you ought to take about eighty dollars and spend it on a very good insurance policy to protect your family. We'll check through the kind of life-insurance programs your employer has and what the union has to offer and between that we will find something that will give your family at least ten thousand dollars' worth of protection. Then you ought to spend the rest of the money in repairing your car and fixing up your house.'

"After, we tell him that we can either be tough or soft, depending on how Joe is reacting. We can either tell him to take it or leave it or argue with him that to continue in his ways is being foolish. The important thing is that we have created a situation which removes that wall between the subject of Joe's personal finances and ourselves. Joe knows that when he goes into a loan company, or goes to buy a car, or anything involving finances that it is customary to discuss his own personal financial conditions. Under those circumstances it is not a violation of his privacy. It is one of those rare situations which permit discussion of personal finances.

"Once the People's Organization has created a situation or what I suppose you could call a medium of education it is up to them to be shrewd enough to be able to exploit that situation for its purpose—education."

A community is not a classroom, however, and the people are not students coming to classrooms for education. The People's Organization must create the conditions and climate in which people want to learn because of the learning itself which is essential to their own life. We have seen one example of the creation of a set of circumstances in the preceding report on the use of the Credit Union to break down the baffling barriers of personal finances. A much more common problem that People's Organizations must concern themselves with is not only providing access to facts but providing them in a manner in keeping with the dignity and the self-respect in all people. People prefer to get things for themselves rather than have them given, and just as the inhabitants of Muddy Flats balked against organization because of their pride,[1] so does the average person possess a latent resentment against having facts given to him on a silver platter. The following report of an organizer working in the field of popular education with a fairly large People's Organization is illuminating on this point:

"Our people lived in shacks and hovels. One of our biggest problems is housing—decent, good housing fit for human habitation. Some of our families live in one-room shacks. Why, take the Joneses. They've got nine children and all of the kids and their parents sleep in one room—because the whole house is just one room. One of the big points in our program is getting running water. Not hot and cold water, but just plain running cold water. Then we have another goal in what we call our long-term program. That goal is—inside toilets. Some people think that it's only when the millennium comes that we'll get 'em. So you see, when we say that one of our big problems is housing, we're not exaggerating.

"Well, lots of us got interested in the government public-housing program. I have been interested in government housing for a long time and while I am not an expert in the field, I know a good many of the answers. Well, we had a big mass meeting and a

[1] See Chapter 7.

special committee was set up on housing. I was put on that committee. There were about sixteen of us. All of the committee members had lots of questions about federal regulations and requirements on housing projects and they were the kinds of questions that I could have easily answered *but I knew that if I gave them the answers they would not like it. By this time most of the guys were good friends of mine and would have gone to hell for me, but they still would have felt sour about my knowing all about it and their knowing nothing. Many a time a guy will disagree with you not because of what you said but because you said it and the way you said it.*[2]

"This is what happened: We all went to the Public Library and got the names of housing pamphlets, then each one of us wrote the government and got copies of the same pamphlet. Then we sat down and we tried to find the answers to our questions in the pamphlet. Remember we would all be reading our own copy of the same pamphlet. I would find the answer on, say, page twenty-two and then I would say, 'Hey, fellows, look at this over here on page twenty-two.' (I would then read the first three or four words.) 'Maybe this is the stuff we're looking for——' Instantly one of the other committee members would say, 'Yeah, look here on page twenty-two,' and then somebody else would start reading it and would be interrupted frequently by the others. Through this interplay of each one reading a bit and directing his companions' attention to a line, or a sentence, or word, the answer to the question was understood by all of them and the understanding was something which they all felt they had gotten themselves.

"After a while I didn't have to do that kind of stuff any more. You see, these people are just the same as the rest of us. The biggest thing we got out of college was to learn where to go to find facts. After that it was up to us to go there and learn. So it is with us here in

[2] My italics.

the People's Organization. Once our people know where and how to get facts they'll do it themselves. And they have been doing it ever since."

One of the most significant educational features of a People's Organization is the fact that its all-inclusive and functional program shatters the shell of isolationism surrounding not only the community but the individuals that make up the community. In the first stages of the building of a community organization local provincial pride is placed upon a pedestal.[3]

As time goes on, the purpose, character, and drive of the People's Organization takes a direction which is the very antithesis of community chauvinism. The People's Organization begins to learn, through its own practices, of the functional relationship between the community, the city, the state, the nation, and the world as a whole. New horizons appear and the People's Organization becomes intensely interested in subjects which had hitherto never been thought of, let alone regarded as having any relationship to the people's lives and experiences.

A graphic illustration of this type of popular education occurred in a powerful People's Organization in Chicago, the Back of the Yards Neighborhood Council mentioned earlier in this book. The Back of the Yards Council had been responsible for the development of the free Hot Lunch and Penny Milk program for schoolchildren in Back of the Yards. This program became a tremendous boon to the health and nutrition of the children. The Hot Lunch project became an integral part of the general program of the Back of the Yards Council.

After some months officials of the Back of the Yards Council were informed that unless the Congress renewed its appropriation for the Hot Lunch project the entire national Hot Lunch program would be

[3] See Chapter 6.

terminated, including that of Back of the Yards. The Back of the Yards Council prepared to battle for its Hot Lunch project. Its officials were fully aware of the significance of the Hot Lunches for the physical welfare of the neighborhood children, but the Back of the Yards Council recognized *that the only way the Back of the Yards Council could continue to have a Hot Lunch project would be for the national Hot Lunch program also to be continued. In order to fight for their own Hot Lunch project they would have to fight for every Hot Lunch project in every part of the United States.*

In order to carry out this fight, leaders of the Back of the Yards Council had to familiarize themselves with the governmental "matching" financial arrangements—the relationships of various departments of the government, such as the Department of Agriculture, to this project—the arguments pro and con on the issue of the appropriation, the governmental channels through which a bill has to proceed before it reaches the floor for a vote—the requirements within the national appropriation for a state subsidy, the securing of facts on the number of Hot Lunch projects throughout the country, and a wealth of other information dealing with government administration. Leaders of the Back of the Yards Council who went to Washington were so completely informed on the issue that many Senators who were opposing the bill were surprised to learn from Back of the Yards leaders that they had such and such a number of Hot Lunch projects in their own states, and that such and such a number of families in their own states were desirous of the continuance of this project. The calm, sound, factual, pithy, and sincere testimony of Back of the Yards leaders before both the Senate and House committees captured the admiration not only of most of the Senators and Representatives, but of a good many of the newspaper correspondents and columnists. The work of the Back of the Yards Council was to a significant extent responsible for the ultimate passage of the appropriation insuring the continuance of the Hot Lunch project.

Immediately after the success in Washington, Back of the Yards leaders went to Springfield and, three days before its scheduled adjournment, the State Legislature had a bill for subsidy drawn up, run through committees, read on the floor, and passed as the last item of business. The knowledge of parliamentary procedures, committee regulations, governmental red tape, legislative floor tactics, and general information on the issue that was put to use by the Back of the Yards leaders evoked the admiration of the state legislators. Today Back of the Yards leaders not only know more about governmental procedures than most professors of civics; they are also completely cognizant of the place of their community in the general mosaic of communities which make up this nation.

Those who have devoted themselves to the building of People's Organization have become more and more convinced that one of the most significant educational approaches is not through argument, through lectures, through logic, or any other conventional common practices but through rationalization. These organizers feel, on the basis of their experiences not only in People's Organizations but in their own general life, that most people in a great many instances act first and think afterward of the reasons why they acted. It seems as though a good part of our knowledge and what we may refer to as our own philosophy and attitudes are not things that we carefully and laboriously think through but are the rationalizations or self-justifications for acts we have already committed.

To many organizers the idea that most learning is done by rationalizing has become a basic premise in the educational programs within the People's Organization. The educational slogan has become: "Get them to move in the right direction first. They'll explain to themselves later why they moved in that direction and that explanation will be better learning for them than anything we can do." A clear illustration of this form of popular education through rationalization occurred in a city located close to the Mason-Dixon line where an organizational campaign involved the getting together of the organized labor movement in one big mass meeting. The organizer had already progressed to the point where he had secured the support of the three major parts of the labor movement: the American Federation of Labor, the Congress of Industrial Organizations, and the Railroad Brotherhood.

During the conference the organizer held with the leaders of these representative labor unions, the Negro problem suddenly loomed in the foreground and became a prime issue. It began when one of the Railroad Brotherhood leaders, in discussing the arrangements for the mass meeting, casually remarked, "And the Niggers will sit up in Nigger Heaven."

The organizer took strong exception to the principle of segregation and was informed by the representatives of the American Federation of Labor as well as the Railroad Brotherhood that this particular town was Jim Crow and as far as they were concerned Jim Crow was right—"After all, a Nigger is a Nigger." The union representatives then went on to point out how "even in our unions the Niggers have their place—and they keep it." The organizer reports the tactics used to solve the issue as well as the ensuing educational process.

"I turned to the C.I.O. leader and said, 'Well, how do you stand on this?' The C.I.O. leader began to hedge around with a lot of general remarks that it wasn't the policy of the C.I.O. to be Jim Crow but after all in a town located so far south they had to respect local traditions and a lot of stuff like that. I realized that I was facing a united front of all three organizations. The first tactic had to be a maneuver to split the ranks of these three labor unions. With that in mind I turned to the C.I.O. leader and said, 'Well, now, I understand that your constitution has a statement that reads something like this: "regardless of race, color, or creed." Is that right?' The C.I.O. leader began to say, 'Yes—but down South——' I interrupted with, 'Well, don't tell me about that; after all, we have no secrets around here and we aren't doing anything we have to keep under the table. As long as we're not doing anything to be ashamed of, let's make a public announcement of our policy. Now, I have three newspaper reporters outside—one from the *Herald*, one from the *Bugle*, and one from the *Press*. I'll call them in and you tell them.'

"The C.I.O. leader flushed, then muttered, 'Well, you don't have to call any newspapermen in. The C.I.O. has always stood against Jim Crow and that's where we stand.' The split had been accomplished.

"I followed through by addressing the A.F.L. leaders. I began, 'The A.F.L. is an independent organization and its policies are completely decided by itself —it has its own autonomy and whatever the C.I.O. wants to do is no business of the A.F.L. Is that right?'

"The A.F.L. leader arose and belligerently said, 'That's right! If the C.I.O. wants to treat Negroes like white men that's their lookout, but by God, whatever the C.I.O. decides on doesn't mean a thing to us.'

"I repeated the same statement to the Railroad Brotherhood and they responded precisely as did the A.F.L.

"Following these expressions of opinion from all three groups I played my ace-in-the-hole. I said, 'Well, now we're completely agreed that each union runs its own affairs. Since the C.I.O. says that they are against Jim Crow and since the A.F.L. and the Railroad Brotherhood say that they are for Jim Crow and since this is a democracy, then there is only one thing to do. We'll split the auditorium in half; the C.I.O. will sit on one side with Negroes and whites and the A.F.L. and the Railroad Brotherhood will sit on the other side and have all the Jim Crow and segregation that they want.'

"There was a momentary silence. The A.F.L. and Railroad Brotherhood leaders exchanged uncomfortable glances. What was in their eyes was as clear as if it had been spoken. 'What a newspaper picture that would make! Black and white faces on the C.I.O. side of the auditorium and a solid wave of white faces on the Railroad Brotherhood and A.F.L. side of the hall! What organizational propaganda that picture would be for the C.I.O. in enlisting Negroes into its membership!'

"After a few moments the A.F.L. leaders looked down at their hands and blurted, 'Aw, let's throw Jim Crow out the window all together—for *this* meeting, mind you.'

"Although this mass meeting, which would be the first one in this town in which there was no segregation, would be a dramatic step forward, nevertheless, the mass meeting was relatively unimportant compared to the speedy rationalization that followed my little talk with the labor leaders. Not one of these labor leaders would admit to himself that he had been tricked or maneuvered into a progressive position. That would be too much of an ego blow. They knew that they had been irrevocably committed to a nonsegregated mass meeting. The rationalization process had begun to operate and, *my,* how those people educated themselves! For the next few days, labor leaders who had been bitterly Jim Crow all their lives came to me saying, 'I think we've done right by throwing over Jim Crow. What the hell, we're living in a democracy, aren't we?' or 'Well, if labor doesn't give the Nigger—excuse me—I mean the Negro a break, where in hell is he going to get it?'

"So it continued and grew—an action which had

been taken purely because of tactical reasons. In the weeks following the mass meeting, classes, forums, and other educational programs on race relations were set up within these unions. This whole educational program originated in the rationalizing self-education that began when these labor leaders had to prove to themselves they were right in opposing segregation and decided to do so on the basis of morality rather than expediency."

In a People's Organization popular education is an exciting and dramatic process. Education instead of being distant and academic becomes a direct and intimate part of the personal lives, experiences, and activities of the people. Committee members find that they must become informed about the field of activities of their committee; they later discover that in order to be capable of carrying out their own activities they must know about all those other problems and activities that are related to the committee's work. The committee that becomes interested in housing shortly finds itself involved in the fields of planning, health, race relations, and many other fields. Knowledge then becomes an arsenal of weapons in the battle against injustice and degradation. It is no longer learning for learning's sake, but learning for a real reason, a purpose. It ceases to be a luxury or something known under the vague, refined name of culture and becomes as essential as money in the bank, good health, good housing, or regular employment.

10

Psychological Observations on Mass Organization

THE ORGANIZATION of people's movements involves both understanding and effective coping with an infinite variety of circumstances and situations. Through conferences and written reports organizers have presented extremely significant aspects of organizational work. The importance of a number of these observations secured in the field cannot be overestimated, but at the same time they do not readily lend themselves to classification within chapters. They fall into what might be thought of as an organizer's notebook. On the whole they tie into the general subject of mass organization as psychological observations on the latter. This chapter will deal with some of these observations that are of great importance in the organizational work of building people's movements.

What They Mean by Their Own

It is impossible to overemphasize the enormous importance of people's doing things themselves. It is the most common human reaction that successful attainment of objectives is much more meaningful to people who have achieved the objectives through their own efforts. The objective is never an end itself. The efforts that are exerted in the actual earning of the objective are part and parcel of the achievement itself. It is all one continuous process. This is so important that the actual definition of the objective itself is determined by the means whereby the objective was obtained. It is the difference in the feeling of a person who purchases a car with his own earnings as against one who receives the car as a gift. No one would dispute that the car means far more to the one who has made sacrifices and purchased it from his earnings. The same psychological reaction universally occurs in human beings toward all things. What you get by your own effort is really yours. It is a part of you, bound and knit to you through the experiences that you have undergone in securing it.

Important as all this is, there is a much more profound basis for the passionate desire of all human beings to feel that they have personally contributed to the creation and the securing of any objective they desire. It is a part of what great religious schools of thought call the dignity of man. It is living in dignity to achieve things through your own intelligence and efforts. It is living as a human being. To live otherwise and not to share in the securing of your own objectives but simply to receive them as gifts or as the benevolent expression of either a government which does not consult with you or as the hand-out of a private philanthropist, places you in the position of a pauper. While to be given life's essentials may be physically pleasant it is psychologically horrible, and the recipient, though outwardly expressing appreciation, is inwardly filled with revulsion.

As we have seen, a People's Organization can arise only from the efforts of the people themselves. Their achievements are meaningful only in terms of their own efforts. They cannot be given anything; they must work for what they get or at least be a link in the chain of events which culminates in the final securing of their objective.

A vivid example of what people mean by *their own* and the appalling lack of understanding among many individuals of the natural human desire of people to have their self-respect and to do things themselves is vividly illustrated in a conversation between Lincoln Steffens and Judge Gary.

He [Gary] said the policy was to give as many as possible of the employees ownership and interest in the company and to increase their pay. It had turned out well for the company. We argued it a bit. I wasn't very serious, and by and by I shunted the argument by asking what he had done as a labor, rather than as a company, leader. He hesitated again before he said: "Well, we have done a lot of welfare work."

"Welfare!" I exclaimed. "You can boast of that? You must know what labor calls that—hellfare work."

"Yes, I know, but I don't understand why."

"I can tell you why," I said, and he seemed really eager to know.

"If you can explain that to me," he said, "you will render me a service, for I have never understood the bitter prejudice of labor against our appropriations for the improvement of shop conditions."

"You don't understand why the wage workers, who want higher wages, are not pleased with cold showers, soap, and clean towels, neat dressing-rooms, lawns, and flowers?" He demurred at my list, but he passed it with a laugh, and accepted my revised question: "You want me to tell you why, when your workers want whatever is coming to them in money for beer, they are not happy when you give it to them in white toweling?"

"Y-y-es," he frowned and smiled. "Yes."

"You have, I hear," I began, "a fine corner apartment in the Waldorf?" He nodded. "Well furnished, to your taste, and a lot of paintings on the walls—all of your choosing, all to your taste?" He nodded; he was a patron of art, and

it was said that he did his own buying and collected pretty good things.

"Do you ever leave your apartment for a vacation?"

Yes, he did.

"Good," I said. "I'll make you a proposition. The next time you are going away for a period, let me know, leave me a sum of money, your own money, and give instructions in the hotel office to admit me to your quarters with permission to do whatever I choose to do."

Puzzled, interested, he screwed up his handsome face and asked, dubiously, "What will you do?"

"I will throw out that terrible furniture you like, and put in what I like, furniture to my taste. I'll take out your rugs and choose carpets in tone with the walls and the room generally. And the pictures—I haven't seen the paintings you have been collecting, but I am sure they are to your taste, not to mine; and I will replace them with good things, art, the sort of work I like. I'll do it all conscientiously, but I will completely alter and really improve the conditions in which you live, making them what I think they should be. And all with your money, the money you are wasting on your taste, which cannot be as good as mine. And—"

"Wait," he said, laughing. "I can't allow that, and even if I did Mrs. Gary would not stand for it. But I get you." He sobered. "That's it, is it?"

"Yes," I said. "That's welfare work." And I told him about a rich employer I had seen a few nights before at the Brevoort restaurant, tipsy himself, but telling some of us that the reason "we won't pay labor more is because they'd drink it all up Saturday and Sunday and be no good for work on Monday." [1]

It is a common feeling among all people that when something is given to you without any effort required on your own part, the gift itself is relatively meaningless. A revealing example of this occurred in May, 1943, in Mexico City. Mexico has a national pawnshop known as Monte de Piedad. This pawnshop is re-

[1] Lincoln Steffens, *The Autobiography of Lincoln Steffens* (New York: Harcourt, Brace, 1930), pp. 692–94.

garded as a tremendous charitable institution and all Mexican guides include it on their conducted tours. There are few tourists who are not deeply impressed by the size of this charitable institution. The Monte de Piedad has no stockholders. Outside of real estate and livestock anything is taken for pawn and no questions are asked—with the exception of large pieces of property such as pianos, sewing machines, and motor cars, which must be accompanied by bills of sale. About one third of the value is given to the owner who can then redeem his property within six months at the low interest rate of one-half per cent per month. If the property is held longer, the interest goes up to two per cent per month.

In May of 1943 President Camacho decided to pay tribute to the mothers of Mexico. He issued a proclamation that every mother whose sewing machine was being held by the Monte de Piedad should have her machine returned as a gift on Mother's Day. There was tremendous joy over the occasion. Here was a gift being made outright without the slightest effort on the part of the recipients. *Inside of three weeks every single one of the sewing machines was back again in the pawnshop.*

A vivid illustration of the significance of what the people mean by their "own" came out of a discussion of the program and budget of a people's movement which took place between one group that included stockbrokers, financiers, and some professional social workers and another group that included some of the main officers of the People's Organization. During this meeting one of the subjects that came up for discussion was the outdoor recreation center built and owned by the People's Organization. A prominent stockbroker pointed out that since there was a substantial sum involved in athletic equipment and such in this recreation center, the People's Organization should have a night watchman and ought to take immediate steps to hire one.

Officials of the People's Organization brushed aside the suggestion with, "But why do we have to have a night watchman?"

The stockbroker continued, "Well, the public park has equipment similar to yours and they have to hire a night watchman to make sure that the people in the neighborhood don't steal things—now do you see what I mean?"

The officials of the People's Organization looked confused for a moment and then burst forth with, "No! We don't see what you mean. The public park doesn't belong to us; it belongs to the public. Our recreation center belongs to us—it's *ours*—and people aren't going to steal from themselves something which belongs to them—which is theirs. The public park belongs to the public—we don't own it; they *need* a night watchman."

The stockbroker looked even more confused. The expression on his face indicated that he thought the People's Organization officials were "slightly nuts" and he dropped the subject.

Another demonstration of what the people mean by their "own" occurred during a general session of the American Prison Association. At this meeting criminologists, social workers, psychologists, sociologists, recreation workers, psychiatrists, and executives of social welfare agencies throughout the country listened intently to speeches by four delinquent boys who were trying to explain why they were uninterested in either attending boys' clubs or participating in social agency programs. These boys repeatedly emphasized that their only interest was "in our own place." One of the speakers later summed up the point of view of the boys as follows:

"It is of fundamental importance that all of us realize what these boys mean when they say 'our own place.' It's a phrase that is easily used and rarely understood. Most people think, from their point of view, that they are giving others 'our own place.' I think I know pretty well what the boys are driving at when they say 'our own place.' They would rather have a dirty store front with very inferior equipment that is really their own—that really belongs to them—a place where they can do exactly as they please, than a ten-million-dollar boys' club in which they are carefully supervised and where, regardless of the most expensive equipment, they have a feeling (and it doesn't matter how carefully the agency attempts to conceal this feeling) that this place is not their own and that they are using it by virtue of the fact that 'We, the donors, have built this building and permit you to use it.' I am sure that you all know the old story of the boys' clubs, settlement houses, and other cases of character-building institutions that are set up within various underpriviliged communities. The donor or his representative formally opens the building and announces that this building is solely for the use of the boys and girls of the community and that the building belongs to them. It's theirs to do with as they see fit. For instance, here is a beautiful one-hundred-thousand-dollar swimming pool and it is all theirs. They may use it any way they want to—that is, of course, between two and four in the afternoon and God help anyone who is caught in there after four! The irony of all this is that the donor actually believes that he has given this property to the local residents and then reacts with surprise and resentment because of what he believes is the 'ingratitude or stupidity' of the local people."

Degree of Participation

There are few human ativities in which words and ideas are more loosely used and glibly accepted than in the field of organization of people's movements. Among the various ideas on different aspects of People's Organizations there is none more misunderstood than that of *popular participation*. One constantly hears of organizations claiming 100 per cent participation. It is almost impossible to listen to any speaker on community organization or community movements without eventually hearing the statement, "Practically all of the people in the community are involved in this work and participate in it."

A critical study of the extent of popular participation in People's Organizations was made, and the findings differed so radically from the prevalent assumptions that the original study was repeatedly checked. Each checkup corroborated the original findings. Conclusions showed that in the most powerful and deeply rooted People's Organizations known in this country the degree of popular participation reached a point varying between 5 and 7 per cent! This in spite of the fact that those making the study fully recognized that the organizations being evaluated were so much stronger and included so many more people who actually participate than all of the other organizations proclaiming "100 per cent participation" that the People's Organizations were really in a class by themselves.

When these findings were first disclosed to a number of leading authorities in community organization fields, their first reaction was that the findings were incorrect. They knew the character and the strength of the People's Organization that had been studied and they felt that such a low percentage of participation was false on the face of it. Further studies were then projected, and in each case the findings again supported the original percentages.

It was then decided that possibly this was a case of the "entire army being out of step except Johnny." The criteria of participation had been set by the measurements of honest common sense. A sample: If a neighborhood person, when questioned about the People's Organization, responded only by saying that he knew about the organization and that his particular

church or labor union belonged to it, then those remarks were deemed as insufficient to define that person as a participant. However, if the person went on
to say, either of his own volition or in answer to other
questions, that he participated in his church or labor
union on discussions of the policies of the People's Organization or that he served on a committee of the
People's Organization or carried out any kind of an
assignment for it, then he was defined as participating.

The same criteria of participation were then applied in a critical examination of a powerful political
machine. This particular machine is nationally known
as one of the most potent and closely knit organizations ever seen in the political history of the nation.
Typical samples of precincts were studied. The precincts consisted of from 350 to 500 individuals. Of
these 350 to 500 people there is usually one precinct
captain, one or two assistants, one family, and maybe
one job holder (there are not enough jobs in any city
administration to pass out one job to each precinct).
Outside of that the only interest or participation on
the part of the precinct residents occurs during a period of three or four weeks at four-year intervals, when
they are bombarded with campaign literature, and
they vote on Election Day. Here and there tickets
for traffic violations and a few taxes are fixed. Including all other sundry services provided by the machine, such as annual political picnics, the degree of
actual participation according to the criteria used in
evaluating People's Organizations ran about one-
fourth of 1 per cent.

Next to be surveyed was a section of the C.I.O. The
C.I.O. acquired a reputation for the extent of rank-
and-file participation of its membership. A sample
study was made of one of the large industries in a city
where the C.I.O. had a closed-shop checkoff and approximately six thousand dues-paying members. Of
these six thousand members the ones that actually
participated were the stewards, numbering around

three hundred. Of the three hundred stewards, roughly sixty attended their monthly meetings. This applied throughout the year except when the contract came to an end and when strike talk filled the air; then, just as the voter on Election Day goes to the poll, so did the rank-and-file member of the union begin to attend union meetings. When a People's Organization is involved in conflict we see the same tremendous participation among the members that wells up in the union at the time of strike or in a political organization at the time of election. Through the year the actual participation in the union approximated 1 per cent.

The same criteria of participation were applied to many of our strongest and most integrated religious institutions. The actual participation in church or parish activities outside of Sunday attendance at church ran considerably less than one-half of 1 per cent.

What we are concerned with here is daily or frequent participation. Robert S. Lynd in his *Knowledge for What?* made an extremely pertinent comment on this point with reference to rank-and-file participation in civic affairs in the city of Moscow, U.S.S.R. There, where the Communist Party is far stronger than it is in any other part of the Soviet Union and where its very character is such that it can exert social and economic pressures upon the individual beyond anything within our own realm of understanding:

This social activism spreads beyond Party members, though the Party remains the instigating nucleus. As a result, something over half the entire adult population of the city of Moscow, for instance, is estimated to be actively engaged in some form of this socially integrative work.[2]

When one realizes the limited extent of actual rank-and-file participation within American organizations it then becomes obvious why a People's Organization

[2] Robert S. Lynd, *Knowledge for What?* (Princeton, N.J.: Princeton University Press, 1939), p. 86.

which includes from 5 to 7 per cent participation is as powerful as it is. In the present-day American scene 5 per cent participation is a tremendous demonstration of democracy. This fact is also a tragic commentary on the unbelievable degree of apathy and disinterest on the part of the American people. Unless the American people are aroused to a higher degree of participation, democracy will die at its roots—the withering disease of apathy in the roots of democracy will eventually cause its death.

Absorbing Aggressions

An organization founded on a limited program covering a limited community will live a limited life. This is borne out in the rise and decline of the multitudes of community organizations throughout the country. Those that survive after their initial dramatic and well-publicized days, continue purely as ghosts of the past, finding their only identity on letterheads.

Program limitations and a limited community sharply spell the disintegration of the conventional community council. This has been brought out in the previous discussion on "Program." As has been also previously pointed out, the program of a People's Organization knows no boundaries, whether geographical, philosophical, or social. Therefore a People's Organization is a constantly growing movement. Its philosophy, analysis of problems, and general objectives are at the very least national in character. This is extremely significant if we look at it from another point of view: namely, the psychological drives of the individuals working within the People's Organization.

Many of the local leaders and their followers become interested in the People's Organization, apart from social altruism, not only because it provides an opportunity for recognition but because it also provides an outlet for individual and organization aggressions. In the first stages of development, a People's Organization is in a fluid state. There are new frontiers toward which the people strive. Because the character of a People's Organization presents no limitations of program or scope of activities it is never confronted with the fatal psychological malady which affects all conventional segmental community councils.

In the conventional community council the frontiers, both in program and scope of activities, become increasingly limited. The room within the organization becomes more confined; officers become more entrenched in their decisions, and the program itself becomes routine and static. There are practically no outlets for the aggressions of the people within the organization. This blockade against the flow of aggressions nullifies the primary function of the organization, which is to serve as a chemically treated funnel through which these aggressions can be transmuted into a dynamic co-operative drive for the community. What happens in practice is that the people, not having the room in which to discharge their aggressions, must of necessity turn these aggressions inward upon the organization itself, resulting in feuds, hostilities, and a general collapse. The people are not conscious of the actual reason for their feuds within their own organization. They will always say that they are differing with their fellow associates because of principles of program, practice, and so on. After all, has any man striven for public office on a program of complete honesty, openly admitting "I am running for the mayoralty, governorship, or presidency [whichever is the case] because I personally want to be mayor, governor, or president. I would enjoy it"?

Both the program and the organizational structure of the People's Organization is designed so that it completely avoids these weaknesses and failures of the conventional organizational procedure.

Thus a People's Organization allows all drives and aggressions continual movement. There are no blocks or barricades which force aggressions to turn inward. Each step forward inevitably involves more problems and also further propels the People's Organization on an onward, upward path where there is, and always will be, ample room at the top. There is no ceiling to a People's Organization; the members of the organization will always have sufficient room to concentrate their energies and drives on going forward instead of having to fight to keep their own place. To be static in a People's Organization is to commit suicide.

Organization Is in the Last Analysis Disorganization

The building of People's Organizations is the creation of a set of realignments, new definitions of values and objectives, the breaking down of prejudices and barriers and all of the many other changes which flow out of a People's Organization. The actual development of these social forces, coupled with the popular education, participation, and reorientation which is part of this whole process, inevitably means significant changes in the attitudes, the philosophies, and the programs of the constituent community agencies as well as the local people. In this sense, the building of People's Organizations with attitudes and purposes that differ from the prior conceptions and attitudes of the local agencies and groups means that during the building process the local groups and agencies must break down their own accumulations of prejudices and feelings, and undergo a period of disorganization in order to make way for the new values and the new philosophies and new purposes. This period of transition is a period of disorganization. It is this phase which is usually one of the critical stages in the life of a People's Organization.

Social Position of the Organizer

The organizer of a People's Organization will shortly discover one simple maxim: *In order to be part of all, you must be part of none.* In dealing with the innumerable rivalries, fears, jealousies, and suspicions within a community the organizer will discover that not only must his own moral standing and behavior be impeccable, but also that he cannot enjoy the confidence—even to a limited degree—of all other groups as long as he is personally identified with one or two of the community agencies.

In one Western community an organizer who held an official position within the C.I.O. was Protestant by religion and a leader in his church club, and his wife was the president of a local women's club. Shortly after beginning his organizational drive this organizer discovered that he had to resign from his church in order to remove certain barriers between himself and representatives of other Protestant churches in the community. He had to resign from the C.I.O. because of suspicion on the part of the American Federation of Labor and the Railroad Brotherhood. His wife had to resign from her women's club because of the rivalry of another women's society. Very shortly this organizer found that he could not be an official member of any of the community agencies. These circumstances do not apply in the same severe fashion to an organizer who comes into a community from the outside.

It has been said that it is impossible to secure the trust of all groups and that the next best position to be achieved is that of being suspected by all. A person in that position at least finds that he is not branded as a tool to establish a "front organization" for another interest group. But he will find that he is the constant butt of rumors, charges, whispering, sly innuendoes, campaigns, libelous and scurrilous statements from all sides. That is part of his job. If he can't take it he should leave the field of organization as quickly as possible.

Relationship Between Organizer and Local Leaders

The organizer should exercise the greatest care to make sure that his relationships with the local leader are secure and solid before he tries to use those relationships as mediums for stimulating organization work. Strong, solid relationships mean that the organizer is defined by the local leader as an intimate friend and that this friendship includes the exchange of personal confidences, affection, and that personal identification which is the basis of all friendships. It should be remembered that those changes in attitudes and directions desired by the organizer on the part of the local people involve a painful process for these people: the shedding of encrusted prejudices and many other firmly fixed points of view. To keep up a personal relationship with the local leader while continuing to try to change these prejudices places an enormous strain upon the relationship. On this point one organizer reports:

"I had spent a long time trying to get Phillip into the organization and finally he decided to join. We were celebrating his decision at one of the local taverns and Phillip said, 'You remember my stomach ulcers? Gee, they were bad!' I nodded and said something sympathetic. Phil continued, 'Well, you know I went to one doctor after another and they were no help. Well, sir, a couple of weeks ago I was talking to Old Jed up the street—you remember Old Jed—he's that hermit who lives in a tarpaper shack near the railroad tracks—' I nodded again. Phil then leaned back and pointing his finger at me said, 'Well, I told

Old Jed about those stomach ulcers and he gave me a prescription to mix up myself. You take so much kerosene, a little bit of coal soot, and about a quarter of a glass of urine. You mix it all up, let it stand overnight, and then drink it three times a day for three days. Well, believe it or not, I made it and drank it, and it sure fixed up my ulcers. They ain't bothered me for a second since then.'

"Well, I asked Phil to give me the exact ingredients that went into it and I carefully wrote it down. He felt pretty pleased, particularly when I told him I was writing it down for the use of others and that I have other friends who have stomach ulcers. I suppose the honest thing to have done was to tell Phil that he was crazy to ever believe in anything like that—let alone do it—but if I had, Phil's feelings would have been so hurt that he would have walked out of the People's Organization and would never have talked to me after that. About six or eight months from now, after Phil and I have gotten to be very good friends I will be able to sit down with him and say something like this:

" 'Phil, do you really think that stuff you were telling me about cured your stomach ulcers? Boy, we sure were suckers even to give it a second thought.' And then start laughing—and I know that Phil will then laugh over it too. But if I told him now, that would be the end of the whole business, and no purpose would be served except the People's Organization would be weakened and any chances I would ever have to straighten Phil out on some things would have gone up the chimney with the coal soot."

11

Reveille for Radicals

AMERICA was a land green, fresh, and young. It was a land rich not only in natural beauty but richer yet in a vision of a noble life which pervaded the earth and the heavens. A dream of unbounded beauty and dignity. Parts of that dream were written down and we called it the Declaration of Independence. Not just independence from the political rule of Britain but independence from slavery of spirit and soul; a future of freedom for man.

Here the first immigrants broke the virgin soil, built their homes, and raised the small white steeples of their houses of worship. Gray smokestacks joined the white steeples. The smokestacks multiplied and grew higher and higher. They belched forth and the clear American dream became smoky and vague. The land that was green became gray, and soot settled over the soul of America. The Industrial Revolution was here.

The American dream was wrought in the fire of the passionate hearts and minds of America's radicals. It could never have been conceived in the cold, clammy tomb of conservatism. The American radical descends from those who begot, nurtured, fought, and suffered for every idea that moved men's feet forward in the march of civilization—the radicals of the world. The hopes and aspirations of the radicals of the world found fruit in the American Revolution. Here in the New World man would find the new life, the new order; even our money carried this message, NOVUS ORDO SECLORUM.

The history of America is the story of America's radicals. It is a saga of revolution, battle, words on paper setting hearts on fire, ferment and turmoil; it is the story of every rallying cry of the American people. It is the story of the American Revolution, of the public schools, of the battle for free land, of emancipation, of the unceasing struggle for the ever increasing liberation of mankind.

The humanitarian idealism of the Declaration [of Independence] has always echoed as a battle-cry in the hearts of those who dream of an America dedicated to democratic ends. It cannot be long ignored or repudiated, for sooner or later it returns to plague the council of practical politics. It is constantly breaking out in fresh revolt . . . Without its freshening influence our political history would have been much more sordid and materialistic.[1]

Throughout this saga run the strains of the song of America's radicals. In this music there is little of tranquility or majesty but much that is stormy and wrathful. It is the martial music of anger, of faith, of hope; it is the battle hymn of the American radical, "The Battle Hymn of the Republic." Its words burn in the hearts of all radicals:

Mine eyes have seen the glory of the coming of the Lord:
He is trampling out the vintage where the grapes of wrath
are stored;
He hath loosed the fateful lightning of his terrible swift
sword;
His truth is marching on.

[1] Vernon L. Parrington, *Main Currents in American Thought*, Vol. III, *The Beginnings of Critical Realism in America, 1860–1920* (New York: Harcourt, Brace, 1930), pp. 285 ff.

The fundamental issue that will resolve the fate of democracy is whether or not we really believe in democracy. Democracy as a way of life has been intellectually accepted but emotionally rejected. The democratic way of life is predicated upon faith in the masses of mankind, yet few of the leaders of democracy really possess faith in the people. If anything, our democratic way of life is permeated by man's fear of man. The powerful few fear the many, and the many distrust one another. Personal opportunism and greedy exploitation link the precinct captain, the mayor, the governor, and the Congress into one cynical family. It is difficult to find the faintest flicker of faith in man, whether one scours the Democrats, from the Southern racist politicians to the Northern corrupt city machines, or one scrutinizes the decayed reactionaries of the Republicans. On the contrary, it will be found that with few exceptions all of these leaders, regardless of their party labels or affiliations, share in common a deep fear and suspicion of the masses of people. Let the masses remain inert, unthinking; do not disturb them, do not arouse them; do not get them moving, for if you do you are an agitator, a trouble maker, a Red! You are un-American, you are a radical!

The past, the glorious past with all of its comfortable familiarity, was rooted in a general surrender of everyday democratic rights and responsibilities of the people. It was founded on masses of people who were and still are denied the opportunity to participate; who are frustrated at every turn and who have been mute for so long that they have lost their voices. Only at rare intervals did this quiet, peaceful, seemingly dead foundation stir and move. These upheavals were the revolutions of men fighting for the opportunity to play a part in their world, for a chance to belong, to live like men.

These masses of people were and are the substance of society. If they continue inarticulate, apathetic,

disinterested, forlorn and alone in their abysmal
anonymity, then democracy is ended. It has been
stated and restated throughout these pages that substance determines struture and that the form of economy and politics will be and always has been a reflection of either the active desires of a democratically minded citizenry or the passive torpor of a people whose innate dignity and strength have atrophied
from disuse, and who will follow slavelike after a dictator. It is irony worthy of the gods that here in the
greatest democracy on earth is found the least concern
over the prime element of democracy—citizens who
shoulder obligations and stand up for their rights. A
people's democracy is a dynamic expression of a living, participating, informed, active, and free people.
It is a way of life that belongs to the people, that
draws its very life blood from popular participation.
Democracy is alive, and like any other living thing it
either flourishes and grows or withers and dies. There
is no in-between. It is freedom and life or dictatorship
and death.

Human beings do not like to look squarely into the
face of tragedy. Gloom is unpopular and we prefer
the "out of sight, out of mind" escape. But there comes
a time when issues must be recognized as issues—and
resolved. The democratic way of life is at stake. You
cannot meet today's crisis tomorrow. You cannot pick
and choose when and what you will do at your personal convenience. You cannot dawdle with history.

We must face the bitter fact that we have forsaken
our great dream of a life of, for, and by the people;
that the burning passions and ideals of the American
dream lie congealed by cold cynicism. Great parts of
the masses of our people no longer believe that they
have a voice or a hand in shaping the destiny of this
nation. They have not forsaken democracy because of
any desire or positive action of their own; they have
been driven down into the depths of a great despair
born of frustration, hopelessness, and apathy. A

democracy lacking in popular participation dies of paralysis.

There are many conditions in America which we are unable to see in their correct perspective. To a significant extent the old saying that "we cannot see the woods for the trees" holds true of the vast majority of us Americans. Gunnar Myrdal in a survey of the American scene that is strongly reminiscent of Tocqueville's classical analysis a hundred and ten years earlier, bluntly stated:

Political participation of the ordinary citizen in America is pretty much restricted to the intermittently recurring elections. Politics is not organized to be a daily concern and responsibility of the common citizen. The relative paucity of trade unions, cooperatives, and other civic interest organizations tends to accentuate this abstention on the part of the common citizens from sharing in the government of their communities as a normal routine of life.[2]

There are other bitter truths that must be faced. The stifling of opportunities for mass participation in America has inevitably meant the throttling of interest in America as such. Social interests have been displaced by selfish interests. The people no longer think as Americans for America. They no longer speak as Americans for America. They speak for their interest cliques. The welfare of their narrow groups completely overshadows any thoughts of national welfare. They speak for "Organized Labor," for "Business," and for the "Farm Bloc." Even assuming that they do speak for all of their membership, which is an erroneous assumption, the total membership of organized labor, organized business, and the farm blocs would certainly not exceed a maximum of twenty million people. Twenty millions organized with the machinery to articulate their desires, but *many more mil-*

[2] Gunnar Myrdal, *An American Dilemma* (New York: Harper & Bros., 1944), p. 717.

lions of Americans who do not speak, have no collective tongue, have no voice, are silent.

It is not the fault of the legislators that they must listen to the twenty million who are organized, for those are the loudest and, with minor exceptions, the only voices in America. It is not the Constitution of the United States that renders the rest of the population inarticulate; what we have is an evil combination of circumstances and conditions that deny and denounce popular participation. It is true that one day every four years Americans can cast their ballot in an election, but it is also true that for more than 1,400 days that intervene between major elections they are blocked from articulating or carrying on the functions and responsibilities of American citizenship.

These are bitter facts and they have embittered millions of Americans. That is the main reason for the appalling lack of desire on the part of masses of Americans for self-education. The hope for democracy lies in not only a participating *but an informed people.* This already deplorable condition continues to deteriorate steadily.

The diverse activities collectively known as "adult education" in America are often laudable strivings to disseminate education among the common people by universities, philanthropic organizations, state and federal agencies, radio companies, or groups of enlightened community leaders. There is still little concerted drive for self-education in civic affairs. There is no spontaneous mass desire for knowledge as a means of achieving power and independence.[3]

Education must be presented to our people in a way that they will find meaningful. But educators must first educate themselves in the art of democratic teaching in a democracy. They must learn to teach and work with people. The enormous importance of

[3] *Ibid.*, p. 713.

the function of educators in the fulfillment of a democratic destiny is second to nothing.

The job ahead is clear. Every conceivable effort must be made to rekindle the fire of democracy while a few embers yet glow in the gray ashes of the American dream. Once it goes out it may take generations before a new fire can be started. The fire, the energy, and the life of democracy is popular pressure. Democracy itself is a government constantly responding to continuous pressures of its people. The only hope for democracy is that more people and more groups will become articulate and exert pressure upon their government. It is short-sighted to attack the few major pressure groups in this country as "dangerous lobbyists" or "un-American," for although these pressure blocs are seeking primarily to further their own interests, their organizing and bringing pressures to bear upon the government is participation and democratic activity which is infinitely more American, more democratic than the dry, dead rot of inactivity, of refusing to become involved in pressure groups. When we talk of democratic citizenship we talk and think in terms of an informed, active, participating, interested people—an interested and participating people is popular pressure!

A people can participate only if they have both the opportunity to formulate their program, which is their reason for participation, and a medium through which they can express and achieve their program. This can be done only through the building of real People's Organizations in which people band together, get to know one another, exchange points of view, and ultimately reach a common agreement which is the People's Program. This is the reason for participation: their reason—their lives and the lives of their children. The universal premise of any people's program is, "We the people will work out our own destiny."

This is the cardinal basis of democracy, and various specific issues are not too important in comparison with the main issue. *Can there be a more fundamental, democratic program than a democratically minded and participating people?* Can man envisage a more sublime program on earth than the people having faith in their fellow men and themselves? A program of co-operation instead of competition?

Faith without hope is short-lived. The People's Organization is the machinery through which the people can achieve their program. The People's Organization carries within it the overwhelming power generated by the people fighting for themselves. Even their leadership is their own, their natural leaders. In their unity they find the strength to break down all of those restrictions of opportunities which have hitherto prevented participation. It is the most invincible army known to mankind—the people on the march. To the people ultimate triumph may be delayed but it cannot be denied.

It is in an all-inclusive People's Organization that people fight and think as people, as Americans, and not as businessmen, workers, Catholics, Protestants, Jews, whites, or colored. A People's Organization inevitably smashes all artificial barriers, sectarian interests, religious, nationality, and racial distinctions. It is made up of people, its program is a people's program, and they think together, work together, fight together, hope together, achieve together, as people.

The issue to be resolved is the creation of a world for the little people, a world where the millions instead of the few can live in dignity, peace, and security. By a little people's world we mean that way of life that is best for the millions of little people who cluster about the thousands of little crossways of America. The final judgment will not be rendered by the few on Madison and State streets in Chicago, but by the thousands who cluster about Forty-seventh and Ashland. It will not come from one of the busiest crossroads of America at Rockefeller Center in New York, but from the little crossroads of St. Mark's Place and Second Avenue. The coming world for the little people will be shaped by the millions of little people who live around the thousands of these little crossways.

Some sincere intellectual believers in democracy voice two major objections to the building of People's Organizations. First, they fear that it is revolution. They forget that democracy is one of the greatest revolutions in the history of man. They forget that the American government was born out of the Revolutionary War and they forget that the birth certificate of these United States, known as the Declaration of Independence, proudly proclaims as a human right, "That whenever any Form of Government becomes destructive of these ends, it is the Right of the People to alter or to abolish it, and to institute new Government, laying its foundation on such principles and organizing its powers in such form, as to them shall seem most likely to effect their Safety and Happiness."

Those who fear the building of People's Organizations as a revolution also forget that it is an orderly development of participation, interest, and action on the part of the masses of people. It may be true that it is revolution, but it is *orderly revolution*. To reject orderly revolution is to be hemmed in by two hellish alternatives: disorderly, sudden, stormy, bloody revolution, or a further deterioration of the mass foundation of democracy to the point of inevitable dictatorship. The building of People's Organizations is orderly revolution; it is the process of the people gradually but *irrevocably* taking their places as citizens of a democracy.

The second objection voiced by those who fear the building of People's Organizations stems from distrust of power in the hands of the people. They fear that the development and building of People's Organizations is the building of a vast power group which may fall prey to a fascistic demagogue who will seize leadership and control and turn an organization into a Frankenstein's monster against democracy. Those who fear this possibility have learned very little from our present historic period. The road to fascism and dictatorship is paved with apathy, hopelessness, frustration, futility, and despair in the masses of people. It is this fear and complete hopelessness on the part of the masses which ultimately make them relinquish all control over their lives and turn the power over to a dictator.

Fascism does not have a chance of establishing itself over a people who are active, interested, participating, co-operating, informed, democratically minded, and who above all have learned through their experiences to have confidence in themselves and their fellow men. They have learned to become self-reliant, and this feeling of self-respect, respect for their fellow men, and confidence in the power of the people which comes out of a People's Organization is actually the strongest barrier and safeguard against fascism which a democracy can possess.

The critics in this case continue to think of democracy only in terms of its form and structure. It is easier to think of democracy in those terms; it is neat and orderly. The other kind of democracy, real democracy, is as disorderly as life itself—it does not hold to a form; it grows, expands, and changes to meet the needs of the people.

The enormous power necessary for the development of democracy and the resolving of those issues which make life unhappy and insecure can come only from an organization of all of the People's Organizations, institutions, and the people themselves. Only through this kind of People's Organization can we secure the invincible strength that flows from the pooling of all the popular pressures inherent within the people and their organizations.

Among all of the life-and-death lessons we can learn from the 1930's and World War II, none is more important than the lesson that no single people's institution, regardless of its strength or size, can resolve the issues facing mankind. The failure of the institutions of the people to solve basic issues is the result not only of their jealous isolation from one another but of the same mental isolationist policy concerning their objectives. They have forgotten that there is no such thing as a single problem, that all problems are interrelated, that all issues are part of a chain of human issues, and that a chain is no stronger than its weakest link.

The labor unions have concerned themselves primarily with their own problem of bettering working conditions within the industrial areas of their nations. They have placed other issues in a very secondary position and frequently concentrated their all on getting higher wages and shorter hours. They have neglected to recognize that political and social action are as important to their ultimate objective as their economic ends; that money is only meaningful in terms of the kind of life, the kind of housing, the kind of security and health which a people can purchase with it.

Organized business has assumed that greater profits would be pretty much of a cure-all, and it has to a major extent ignored the fact that the welfare of business rests upon the welfare of the consumers of a nation; that business or free enterprise will function in a democracy only so long as the democracy functions.

Organized religion has too often followed the road of other people's institutions. It has made adjustments, compromises, and surrenders to a materialistic civilization for the benefit of material security in spite of occasional twinges of conscience and moral protests. The result has been that today much of organized religion is materialistically solvent but spiritually bankrupt. Laski, the philosopher of the British Labour Party, commented:

It is not enough for them to profess the acceptance of the Christian ethic. In its operation, that ethic has accommodated itself to slavery at its ugliest, to capitalism in its most ruthless form, to every war that has been waged since Constantine made Christianity the official religion of the Empire.[4]

Sectarianism and the pursuit of particular objectives without recognition that life cannot be approached in terms of individual parts have brought havoc to those people's institutions which persist in accommodations, compromises, and surrender on all issues except those which they interpret as their own particular spheres of activity. These practices have insured their survival in structure, but if continued will insure the demise of their substance. Jacques Maritain stated that: "It was not given to believers faithful to Catholic dogma but to rationalists to proclaim in France the rights of man and of the citizen, to Puritans to strike the last blow at slavery in America, to Atheistic Communists to abolish in Russia the absolutism of private profit."[5]

This statement implicitly asks the fearful question, Why? Why was not the Catholic Church in the forefront of the French Revolution for the rights of man and of the citizen? Why was it not a leader in the attack on slavery in America? Why was the Russian Orthodox Church not only absent in the revolt against tyranny and the absolutism of private profit; why was it not in the vanguard of the Revolution? These questions keep recurring.

There is one lesson that came out of the catastrophe of the Second World War which we had better remember, for if we do not, a recurrence of the catastrophe will not leave a sufficient number of us alive to relearn and profit by this lesson. The words of this

[4] Harold J. Laski, *Faith, Reason, and Civilization* (New York: Viking, 1944), pp. 122–23.

[5] *Christianity and Democracy* (New York: Scribner's), p. 38.

lesson were written in the bombed-out buildings and the broken hearts and bodies of Europe. Europe possessed a militant labor movement far stronger than that of America—yet fascism and war came to Europe. Thirty-three million people were involved in the co-operative movement in Europe—yet fascism and war came to Europe. The organized Christian Church is much older and much more entrenched in Europe than in any other part of the world—yet fascism and war came to Europe.

Organized religion, organized labor, and all other organized institutions of the people were completely impotent in preventing fascism and war. We must learn from this, and learn it now, that only in the united effort of all People's Organizations working together in concert lies hope of peace, security, and happiness. Only in the pooling of all the strength of every people's institution and in the awakening of our people to participation lies hope of salvation on earth!

This, then, is the job ahead. It is the job of building broad, deep People's Organizations which are all-inclusive of both the people and their many organizations. It is the job of uniting, through a common interest which far transcends individual differences, all the institutions and agencies representative of the people. It is the job of building a People's Organization so that people will have faith in themselves and in their fellow men. It is the job of educating our people so that they will be informed to the point of being able to exercise an intelligent critical choice as to what is true and what is false. It is the job of instilling confidence in men so that they are sure they can destroy all of the evils which afflict them and their fellows, whether unemployment, war, or other man-made disasters. It is the greatest job man could have—the actual opportunity of creating and building a world of decency, dignity, peace, security, happiness; a world worthy of man and worthy of the name of civilization. This is the job ahead.

The building of these People's Organizations and the achievement of popular participation cannot and will not be done by denouncing the present deplorable condition of democracy. It will not be done by wailing self-recriminations. It can be done only by setting ourselves to the dirty, monotonous, heart-breaking job of building People's Organizations. It can be done only by possessing the infinite patience and faith to hang on as parts of the organization disintegrate; to rebuild, add on, and continue to build.

It can be done only by those who believe in, have faith in, and are willing to make every sacrifice for the people. Those who see fearlessly and clearly; they will be your radicals. The radical will look squarely at all issues. He will not be so weighted down with material or malignant prejudice that he can only look upward with a worm's-eye view. He will not look down upon mankind with the distorted, unrealistic, ivory-tower bird's-eye view, but will look straight ahead on the dead level, seeing man as a man. Not from a long distance, up or down, but as a man living among men.

Let it sound, then. Let it come, clear, strident, ringing, and heart-stirring. Let it come, the rallying cry of America. From the historical "Don't tread on me" to the grim "Tyranny, like Hell, is not easily conquered," to "John Brown's soul goes marching on," to "You shall not crucify mankind on a cross of gold," to "Solidarity Forever!"

These are a few of the past battle cries of the American dream. Let the cry sound again, clearly, boldly, shattering the deathlike silence of decay. Let it reach every corner of America and let its echoes go beyond and shake the hearts of oppressors everywhere. Let it come so that the Western plowman will stop, wipe the sweat from his brow, and, looking up into the bright skies, see the same American vision that will come to the eyes of the millions who dwell in dingy

New York tenements, to the sharecroppers of the South, to the rubber workers of Akron, to the shipbuilders and lumber workers of the Northwest, to the packinghouse workers of the Midwest, and to all the people of these United States. Sound it now. Whether it be the hoarse voice, the bell, the written word or the trumpet, let it come. Sound it clear and unwavering. REVEILLE FOR RADICALS!

Afterword to the Vintage Edition

TODAY while most of the world is working and fighting for the basic means of physical survival, we are locked in battle for our spiritual survival. Theirs is the confrontation with the age-old issues of food, shelter, disease, and the protection of personal property, whereas we are now engaged in the historic confrontation with self.

Probably at no time in American history have we experienced a greater revolution than we now find ourselves facing. This is not a time of change but of cascades of change.

We Americans have led the way into a technological world where in an age of automation, computers, cybernetics, mass media and mass everything, we find ourselves bulging with production surpluses of everything, including time. We find ourselves in a world where people are dying of malnutrition while here most of us are dieting. Even so, our present affluence and achievements are probably minimal compared to our vast productive potentials. According to the Protestant ethic we have been rewarded for our virtue of working for success. In our pursuit of material happiness we have achieved plentitude. We have "security." We—more than three-quarters of us—have it pretty well made when it comes to food, housing, and other physical needs. Even our own minority poor generally need not fear actual starvation or being totally without shelter. And after all, we even have plans to get rid of poverty itself. The only things from the past which continue to operate, as they always will, are the elementary laws of physics—such as *every positive carries a negative*.

Yet, while we seem to have found the good life we also seem to have lost ourselves. We should be happy, but we are in fact confused, frustrated, resentful, and frightened of the feeling of an ever growing loneliness. We don't know what to do because we don't know what's wrong, except that we know that something very fundamental is wrong; something is missing which we know is more important than many of the things we have achieved. That something is a sense of ourselves as individuals, as people, as members of the human family. What is at stake is our sanity. Our world is so fractured in every area and at every level that all the different pieces, seemingly so important in themselves, swirl and beat upon us so that we no longer know what anything means.

Much has been written about what threatens us as residents in this paradise of plenty. The mass media, particularly television, have so transformed communication that, coupled with the interlocking political and economic interests of all mankind in an ever shrinking world, the new technology spells the end of any closed system of ethics. It means that a whole realm of morality and principles must emerge if there is to be any world at all. Remember that it was Aristotle who originated the word *principle*, and he would have been the first to recognize that if fifteen different people from fifteen different backgrounds of experience entered the same room we would find fifteen different sets of principles clogging all attempts at communication.

Similarly we find definitions of truth ranging from Plato through all of the philosophers of history. The president of the jewelry firm Cartier's recently defined truth as, "Now, I felt that in this era of ours, which is certainly characterized by a search for truth, I could be instrumental in presenting the Cartier merchandise to a wider number of customers, many of whom are feeling a great need for truth and find themselves confronted by realities that are creating a new sense of values . . ." Fine gems and precious stones ". . . represent truth in its purest form. They have withstood the vicissitudes of nature for thousands of years and so represent the unquestioned element of purity in a different period." *

In reading this statement one begins dimly to grasp the degree to which interests and experiences define values. Unquestionably the president of Cartier's is speaking for a sector of this affluent society. When such visions of truth are offered us, an organizer must have a deep sense of humor in order to retain his balance and direction in this "civilized" world.

Obviously certain common ethical definitions have to be agreed to. We must accept open-ended systems of ethics and values, not only to meet the constantly changing conditions but also to keep changing ourselves, in order to survive in the fluid society that lies ahead of us. Such systems must be workable in the world *as it is* and not unrealistically aimed toward *the world as we would like it to be.*

Keeping in mind the universal law mentioned earlier that every positive having its corresponding negative, we may well reflect on the fact that the very roots of security, of stability, can and have been anchors of stagnation and rot, holding and dragging us against the winds and seas of change.

* *The New York Times*, August 27, 1967.

We have entered a mass civilization which carries with it a climate of conformity and consensus and which, Ortega y Gasset warned, "crushes beneath it everything that is different, everything that is excellent, individual, qualified and select." The mental overcast resulting from these clouds of consensus looms as one of the most ominous threats for the days ahead.

To face the days ahead we must ask two questions: first, "Where are we?" and second, "Where do we go from here?" We Americans seem to have forgotten where we came from, we don't know where we are, and we fear where we may be going. We are a scene of frenetic fears, confusion, and madness. Scared New World.

Life has become a catalogue of crises: the Urban Crisis, the Race Crisis, the Campus Crisis, the Poverty Crisis, the World Crisis, the Crisis of a Free and Open Society, and underneath it all our personal crises of whether to live or drop out. We are bombarded with so-called studies and reports on the consequences of urbanization, the population explosion, the changing character of our educational system, our values, our family life, our relationships with one another, or rather our lack of relationships, the ever increasing alienation of the individual from his society, his inability to act on those issues that are vital to him, his family, and his community. Sociologists chorus the prevalence of *anomie*, and speculate on what we can do about it.

Already there is much discussion of the idea that "work" as we have known it may well become an economic artifact, as remote from us as the activities of the cavemen. The big concerns now are how we will cope with massive chunks of leisure time, where the jobs will come from as cybernetics moves in, and how to make work meaningful. The nature of jobs is changing from production for profit to service for use. Ultimately most people may be employed exclusively to provide services for one another—which evokes a horrible fantasy unimagined by any pessimistic science-fiction writer concerned with the possibility of a cold impersonal world.

That we look upon these crises as problems is a hopeful sign. A problem is something you can do something about. We may not know how, where, and what, but we know that eventually we can do something. The tragedy would be if we viewed a crisis as a plight; as an inevitability of life, like death; as a happening to which one is resigned. *This has always been the prime task of the organizer—the transformation of the plight into the problem.* The organizer must be able to communicate and convince the people that, if they find a way to join together, they need not fatalistically accept their plights but will have the power to affect the shape of their world. It is then that a people drop their defenses—for instance, the bitter humor that is often the only recourse if man has to live with the inevitable—and begin to act with anger, purpose, and hope.

Today the signs are flying that the American people are ready for organization and for action to "break out" and get back on the road to life, to being free citizens and not alienated bits of anonymity. We are in a revolution and should be reminded of Kropotkin's comment on the Russian Revolution, "The hopeless don't revolt, because revolution is an act of hope."

Let us take a look at a couple of these "crises"; the urban and racial crises.

America's urban crisis is primarily an umbilical crisis. We concede the unprecedented, sweeping and shatteringly rapid changes of our times. We have been ripped from the womb of the past. We know, we see, we hear, we talk about this whole changed and changing world but we will not cut the cord of the past and go out to live in the present. The past, though dead, has the security of familiarity, and so we move like zombies.

Our urban crisis is many-faceted: residual, overlapping local authorities of the past; the flight of whites and industry away from the city; the massive migration to the cities of low-income newcomers—both white and nonwhite; the huge increase in the black population of America's major cities, with all its attendant problems in the areas of education, housing, jobs, and new political alignments.

The tension has added new clichés to the American language: for instance, "the long hot summer" and "confrontation." We are always having a "confrontation," or avoiding a "confrontation." In fact, we have rarely confronted an issue unless we have been driven to a point of no avoidance. The use of force by the authorities against today's wide-spread violence does not represent a real facing up to issues—the current confrontation is the unavoidable reaction to the action of the black ghettos.

Our present impasse on the race issue is due largely to our refusal to confront the issue for one of two reasons: either we don't know what to do about it, or, if we do know, we don't want to do anything. We shun meeting the issue head-on by relying on a series of tired gambits in the form of conferences, surveys, investigations, or study commissions appointed by the president, or governor, or mayor. Then we militantly and self-righteously proclaim our determination for bold, prompt, massive action, which always turn out to be bumbling, procrastinating, minuscule gestures. Blue-ribbon commissions always give birth to blue babies.

I suggest that those who live in the past don't want a confrontation with the present. I believe that white Americans welcome the present race violence and that under the surface reactions of horror and shock is very deep relief. Now white Americans are back in the familiar jungle. Now the confrontation is in terms they can understand and in accord with their prejudices. Now they can have a confrontation because they think they know the answer to violence, and the answer is force, and furthermore they welcome the use of force. Now they no longer have to talk or think about injustice, guilt, or the immorality of racism. Now it is simple: "Law and order must be upheld before we get around to anything else."

The issue we face is not just *what* is to be done, but *how* it is to be done. The situation is far too complex for us to attempt to continue the old practices, which I branded years ago as "welfare colonialism." Democracy can no longer be paraded under the simple disguise of admitting black-skinned representatives, who more often than not represent no one but themselves, to the privy councils. The new Uncle Talk-Toughs who have replaced the former Uncle Toms will be just as ineffective as long as they represent no larger group than the latter did in the past.

The void of leadership in the black ghettos or, similarly, in the white ghettos or the gilded ghettos of the middle class—in short, the general lack of leadership in America—is ominous for the democratic future. The democratic process cannot function without the essential mix of legitimate representatives who can meet with accredited representatives of other sectors of society in order to face up to the pushing, hauling, dealing and temporary compromises that are part of the pressure of democracy. Without this kind of representation the democratic process comes to a halt. This is what is happening today. Where are the leaders of the black ghetto who truly bear the credentials to represent their communities?

Let me put it another way. Suppose that white society, the establishment, the status quo, the power structure or any other name you wish to put on it, awoke one morning after experiencing a divine revelation and said, "Everything we have done in the past as far as our nonwhite fellow citizens are concerned has been hypocritical, immoral, undemocratic, and has violated the Judeo-Christian moral precepts. We have behaved as a superior racist colonial power and regarded our black ghettos as colonies of primitive inferior natives. We have arbitrarily imposed upon them our ideas of programs to 'civilize' them. We have sent down our colonial agents in the form of settlement-house workers, delinquency workers (on the street, over or under the streets), recreation workers, health, education, religious, and other varieties.

"We have bought out those whose intelligence and aggressiveness might have meant trouble. This welfare-colonialism policy helped to assuage our guilt so we could congratulate ourselves on being honest, moral, and democratic while being dishonest, immoral and anti-democratic. Furthermore, ours has been a zoo-keeper mentality of keeping the animals quiet or, to make it sound nicer, of maintaining law and order. We have not only shafted the blacks but insisted that it was for their own good and that they must also like it!

"But now we have experienced the incredible divine revelation and within the hour (before its effects wear off) we say, 'We have been wrong! From now on we will accept our nonwhite neighbors as full equals with full access to every right, opportunity, and freedom enjoyed by whites. They will sit with us as equals at the decision-making table, representing their people.'"

We could then turn to the black ghettos and say, "Send us your representatives." Who would come forth? Who represents these people? Certainly practically none of those whom white society is now consorting with and also financing. Now we see why it becomes so terribly important that the ghettos be organized. Organization is not only for the purpose of power,* but unless a people have become organized and their membership roster is open for public inspection, unless they have met in convention, agreed

* Webster's Unabridged Dictionary defines power as "the ability to act."

upon policy, programs, constitution, and elected officers, you will not find that necessary combination of circumstances from which legitimate, bona fide, accredited representation can be either selected or elected. Across the nation our ghettos are appallingly lacking in those combinations or organizations that can claim to legitimate representation.

The danger of black power is that there may be no black power. This nation desperately needs the organized power of our black sector and its representatives in our body politic. I am gravely concerned that those who talk black power will do no more than talk, will not engage in the arduous, tedious job of organization. If this happens the term "black power" will degenerate from a proud, meaningful phrase and threat into a joke.

Certainly the basis for real power cannot be found among most of those whose vocabulary and mentality are restricted to simplistic two-word slogans, "Black Power" and "Get Whitey." These people, with their frenetic but unproved claims that they represent the ghetto, bring to mind the story of the emperor's new clothes.

Today there is a great emphasis among blacks on identity: black culture, black history, and pride of race—"Black is beautiful." The importance of achieving the objective of a black sense of identity cannot be understated. It is essential and of prime significance. It must be achieved. What concerns me deeply is that identity without power is still a second-class identity. Black culture must proceed hand-in-hand with the organization of blacks for black power. Actually most lessons of life are learned in and through action. Many of the blacks who are most articulate about black culture have yet to demonstrate their capabilities for organization. For many of them the evocation of black culture has become a comforting rationale, an escape to avoid being put to the test of organization. They say that blacks are not ready for organization until they have achieved their black identity. What they mean is that they either cannot organize or are afraid to try and fail. In my personal experiences I have never met a competent organizer who could resist organizing in any situation that demanded power for the sake of effecting change. Any organizer, educator, or sophisticated person knows that a basic, personal sense of identity can come only through the drama of moving experiences—of action. It is the change which occurs within a black minister of a small church living in a drastically limited segregated world, who because he is a leader of a real, not theoretical, black power organization and because of the actions attentant on that position, finds himself within a period of two years at an annual stockholders' meeting confronting the chairman of the board of one of the nation's largest corporations. He is not only confronting this chairman and issuing an ultimatum, but is followed by the nation's press as he storms out of the meeting. His actions are looked upon by the mass media as more important than what is happening at the stockholders' meeting. He has achieved his identity, his black identity. He is a man in every sense and he achieved his manhood the only way any man gets it—through action. And he has power. Black culture without black power is still castration. We are witnessing the emergence of a variety of species, including one which I have described as "the black in the gray flannel dashiki." We must have more black organizers who will do the job.

Another problem of today is the breakdown of communication between blacks and whites. If whites believe in full equality and the essential dignity of all races, then they cannot surrender their own dignity and be part of the masochistic cult which submits to outrageous and, in many cases, patently psychotic charges and attacks. A relationship of dignity and equality cuts both ways, and no one who is committed to the full equality and dignity of others can or will sacrifice his own in the process. During the recent trial of Black Panther leader Huey Newton, many San Francisco white liberals wore large buttons reading "Honkies for Huey!" Can you imagine if a white civil rights leader were on trial that blacks would go about with buttons reading "Niggers for ———!" Of course not. So long as mindless white masochism and unproductive, groveling guilt prevails, so long will there not be any meaningful communication or constructive positive changes for a world of equality. Many whites have become terrified of even raising a question with blacks for fear of having it branded as a race issue. Unless whites overcome their own hangups so that they can both listen and speak to blacks in the same way that they would be listening and speaking to whites, and vice versa, we will continue to face the consequences of black charlatans combining with white neurotics to sow the seeds of disillusionment and bitterness, and we will provide a comforting rationale for all racial bigots, both black and white.

The lack of citizen organization in the black ghettos is common in most of the other communities that make up the city. Our most populous cities have little citizen participation, little effective local democracy, and the individual has little, if any, degree of self-determination.

The plight of the people in our cities, is made worse by a network of "citizen committees," "Health and Welfare Councils," "Poverty Program Committees," and other blue-ribbon packages that claim to represent people who have given them no mandate and who, as often as not, are ignorant that others are speaking in their name.

Without questioning the undoubted integrity and sincerity of those involved, I believe great harm has been done to the city and its people by these tiny organizations of professionals from private and government agencies who, along with an occasional other nonresident, claim to be spokesmen for hundreds of thousands of people throughout the city. The unchallenged presence of these small groups creates the impression that the population is being democratically represented. No number of "citizen committees," "Health and Welfare Councils," or other such devices can successfully play stand-in for the real thing. Unrepresentative committees are not democratic by virtue of ritual.

Misinformed as to the true state of affairs, people who are honestly searching for ways to allay the cities' multiplying woes turn to mechanical solutions. Mechanical solutions will not do the job. The truth is that when the people of a great city find the avenues of self-expression cut off, the results are that the political, economic, and social channels clog up and backfire. It is highly undemocratic to plan, govern, arrange, and impose programs without communication with the people for whom they are designed; it is also disastrously impractical.

Other cities are rapidly emulating New York's unique and gigantic welfare industry. A book of more than four hundred pages is needed merely to list New York's social and welfare agencies. The welfare establishment has mushroomed to the extent that it must now be classified as one of urban America's major industries. So many thousands of people and millions of dollars may be an incalculable asset, but may also pose a singular problem, if the industry pursues a course that is self-protective and either irrelevant or in contradiction to the wishes and demands of the people.

With the current poverty program and other federal operations, public funds are used to supplement and support the budgets of many "private" agencies. The practice blurs the line between the public and private domain. Those of us committed to volunteerism as a basic concept in democracy are seriously concerned with the implications involved in this arrangement.

Our cities lack citizen participation or organization on the local level. The failure of the "bottom" to make itself felt has permitted city-wide institutions and major interest groups—whether welfare, economic, religious, service, or fraternal—to arrogate the power of speaking for individuals without any challenge or objection. With the urban society's development of vertical city-wide organizations and agencies, the disappearance of an articulate and active mass base has in effect insulated the heads of these organizations from their bodies.

This lack of citizen participation on local levels has resulted in walls of isolation and secular barriers between many of the organizations in the local community. These walls extend upward in social skyscrapers through the life of the city, but there are no elevators running from bottom to top, so that the different institutions are separated to a degree ominous for a democratic future.

In the local community the individual citizen generally reacts to this situation by not reacting. Caught in circumstances that make him feel a lack of identification as an individual, which gives him a numbing sense of *not* belonging and a feeling that no one really cares for him, he responds by not caring. In the course of my work I have talked to people in just about every kind of American community, and nowhere is the old slogan "You can't fight City Hall," uttered with as much conviction as in these cities.

Even when a person may have a sudden desire to take a hand, he lacks the means by which to translate his desire into active participation. And so the local citizen sinks further into apathy, anonymity, and depersonalization. The result is his complete dependence on public authority and a state of civic-sclerosis.

I do not believe that democracy can survive except

as a formality if the ordinary citizen's role is limited to voting, and if he is incapable of initiative or all possibility of influencing the political, social, and economic structures that surround him. This issue is at the center of the future of democracy in America.

The breakdown of citizen activity at the local level has fostered a phenomenon foreign to basic American premises. The concentration and centralization of power, authority, and office in the hands of a few has reached an unprecedented highwater mark in city, state, and national government.

I am fully aware of the dangers of a parochial and isolationist mentality. I have seen too many examples of community chauvinists, of jingoistic local groups doing things without consulting the common good. I am painfully cognizant that modern city problems require intricately co-ordinated planning if they are to be solved. I know, too, that meeting our city problems satisfactorily means making certain sacrifices for the general well-being.

Bearing this in mind I nevertheless recall Alexis de Tocqueville's observation that in the last analysis democracy is preserved and strengthened by maintaining differences and variations. When—as is happening in our cities—all strong, local vested interests are obliterated, when these differences are removed, then I too see what Tocqueville saw as the major peril to our democracy: an egalitarian society that may have the look and forms of democracy, but is its very opposite.

The current American scene can be lamented for its violence, crime, and chaos. To me there is less violence today than there was in the period that saw lynchings, murder of labor organizers, mobster rule of the cities in the Prohibition period, the Memorial Day Massacre by Chicago's police in the late 1930's, and the sinister everyday violence of whites against blacks. We dare to talk about the violence of the ghetto riots, which mainly consist of an assault against property, when for these hundreds of years we have daily, hourly, visited upon the blacks a violence against human spirit, a degradation and denial reminiscent of Chinese torture. What makes it even worse is our inordinate hypocrisy in posing as protagonists of freedom, equality, and fraternity while denouncing totalitarian racist butchers. Phony self-righteousness makes us grotesque.

What many see as chaos and disorder today are to me the boiling over of the human spirit in a demand for direction and purpose to give meaning to life and carry us toward the goals of freedom, equality, economic security, opportunity, justice, and peace.

Our world has always had two kinds of changers, the social changers and the money changers. History is made up of the constant conflict between the two—witness the renowned account in the New Testament of Christ in the temple.

The social changers go by many names: agitators, revolutionaries, catalysts, and "outside" trouble makers.* We have added still another cliché to our vocabulary: "The generation gap."

True, the older generation does not look particularly hopeful. They were the young radicals of my time, the late thirties, forties, and fifties, and with rare exception have moved over into the establishment. Where they have not moved over as individuals they have been carried along by organizations which were formerly radical and today are part of the establishment. Many protested when their organizations went to the right but they stayed with them. They professed their desires to remain to the left and pro-

* The establishment, the status quo, the power structure, or the lousy bastards, depending upon one's point of view and vocabulary, has always identified all trouble makers, agitators, revolutionaries, etc., as being from the "outside." Generally speaking, there is a certain validity to this, since the power establishment usually has retained power by crippling, crushing, or corrupting any would-be developing social changer within its area of power.

claimed their anguish at being seduced, but no one has ever been seduced who didn't want to be. Many of them claim to be "forward-looking" on the basis of a record of past progressivism. They continue to look at their past and stumble backward into the future, unseeing, confused, bitter and resentful at their rejection by the present generation. They rationalize in defense of themselves, which inevitably leads them to a defense of the establishment that may border on the absurd.

Many of the predictions I made some twenty years ago in *Reveille for Radicals* have, to my intense regret, been fulfilled. An example of this is to be found in the organized labor movement, which today is a part of the establishment and not even the progressive part at that. My comments then about the Building Trades Unions could have been written today; these unions are still segregated. What could be more absurd than the head of the now-merged A.F.L.-C.I.O., George Meany, defending the criminal idiocy of Vietnam.

Mr. Meany also said that the "one overriding fact" that "is and must be the primary concern of the A.F.L.-C.I.O." on the Vietnam war was the existence of a free trade union movement in South Vietnam. He said he could not understand any unionist who would advocate a course that would abandon those union members "to certain destruction."

"And, perhaps, I am too simple to comprehend how one who takes that position can be called a 'liberal,'" he said. "But the A.F.L.-C.I.O. is a very large house—with many mansions—and it takes all kinds." *

Mr. Meany's only flash of insight is in his words ". . . perhaps, I am too simple to comprehend . . ."

In *Reveille for Radicals* I criticized organized religion as having

* *The New York Times*, December 8, 1967.

. . . followed the road of other people's institutions. It has made adjustments, compromises, and surrenders to a materialistic civilization for the benefit of material security in spite of occasional twinges of conscience and moral protests. The result has been that today much of organized religion is materialistically solvent but spiritually bankrupt.

These words could just as well have been written twenty-three minutes ago instead of twenty-three years ago. A few years ago we witnessed a commitment, a leadership and great contribution by organized religion at the beginning of the civil rights revolution, but this burst of energy seems to have waned, and today the churches are hung up in two different directions. First, the former militant leadership has submitted to an abnormal, indefensible masochism which makes them willing victims of cynical black extremists who say, "Give us your money and be grateful that we are taking it, and get away from us until we call on you for more money."

It is these same church people who are now indulging in the new game of having white racism seminars and paying high premiums for the most insulting and sickest blacks to come and defecate all over them. It is the kind of gambit best understood by those who are familiar with the Marquis de Sade's flagellation. And yet one must realistically raise the question, "Can there be such a compounding of guilts and neuroses wherein the white church leaders would give money under these circumstances?" What seems to come through, at least to the writer, is that white church leaders privately are welcoming the extremist separatist rejection from these particular articulate blacks (who are certainly not leaders in the sense that they have a following) as an esape hatch, as a way to cop out of the whole scene by saying. "After all, that is what they want and we respect their dignity and independence, and therefore the only thing we can do is give them the money and then withdraw."

On the other side are those large segments of the churches, both the membership and their ordained representatives, who at this point feel that they have had it. They are tired of the whole issue and they, too, now have the rationale that after all the blacks don't want them and they are not going to impose themselves where they are not wanted; they are now back in their old ritualistic rut.

The church today is even worse off than it was twenty years ago. When one is faced with the extraordinary scene of the Catholic Bishops of America in their national conference avoiding taking a position on a specific situation such as the grape workers' strike in southern California, then "prudence" becomes the stench of decay.

The church is also at the crossroads. Many of the rebellions within the churches proper find their roots in the present revolutionary, technological age that has led to the development of mass media and the crumbling of all barriers to communication and mobility as well as nature's other obstacles to immediate, close contact within the human race. The days of closed ethical systems are gone. The peoples of the world must live together, and the world is shrinking by the hour. Living together means that the multiple ethical systems and values around the earth must be synthesized into certain universals acceptable to the people of the world. This becomes another fundamentally important problem that the church now faces. It means that the church must work through to the construction of an open-ended system of ethics and values—as I stated earlier—able not only to meet the constant changes of these times but sufficiently flexible to continue changing so as to survive in the fluid society ahead of us. Most important, it must be an ethical system which will be workable in the world as it is and not, as in the past, be aimed toward the world as we would like it to be. Unless this construct of ethics is one which can be lived up to in the world as it is, it will be unacceptable to the people of the world.

In essence what I have been saying here is that the church must now address itself to its role of being a vital catalyst in creating those circumstances which will combat the darkness of depersonalization and conceptualization. It must play an important part in the creation of those political, social, and economic circumstances whereby people will have the ability to act and the power to operate as free citizens in a free society so that our present civilization will not die. The central question that the church of today and tomorrow must face is no longer, "Is there life after death?" but rather, "Is there life after birth?"

The younger generation is almost as discouraging as the older. Despite its "campus crises" and multitudinous minor "confrontations"—many seemingly for the sake of confrontation—this generation may well be later described by history as the dropout generation. Here we find dissent by dropout which takes a number of forms.

At one extreme we have the hippies, who have not only physically and mentally dropped out but have even passed further into social outer space by taking their "trips" with drugs.

On the other side we have the so-called activists, who in their own way are also out of the action. By refusing to begin with the world as it is and to build power instruments for change, they have reacted with a disorganized, almost anarchistic, approach of "confrontations" and "doing their thing."

The tragedy of the young generation's "radicals" is that they dogmatically refuse to begin with the world as it is. But the only world we have is the world as it is, and we have to begin with that.

Any social changer, throughout history, has always known that you begin from where you are. Change can only be effected through power, and power means organization. Organization can be built only around issues which are specific, immediate, and realizable. Phrases like "participatory democracy" are meaningless for the purpose of real organization.

When we begin with issues we begin with controversy. There is no such animal as a "noncontroversial issue"; in fact, it is a contradiction in terms. When you and I agree about something, we have no issue; it is when we disagree that "the issue is drawn."

A book I am now completing presents certain universal rules of change.* The first one reads, "Change means movement. Movement means friction. Friction means heat. And heat means controversy." It is as simple as that. The same rule that applies in the mechanics is even more germane to social mechanics: movement means friction. The only places where one can have movement without friction is either in outer space, which is friction-free, or in a graduate seminar of a university, or in a church conference that emphasizes reconciliation. "Reconciliation" as the term has been used is an illusion of the world as we would like it to be. In the world as it is "reconciliation" means that one side has the power and the other side gets reconciled to it. Then you have reconciliation and peace and co-operation.

The fact that we accept working in the world as it is does not in any sense negate, dilute, or vitiate our desires to work toward changing it into the world as we would like it to be.

There is a great difference between the world as it is and the world as we would like it to be. One way to see this quickly is to turn on television early any evening and watch drama follow drama, in each of which love and virtue always emerge triumphant. This world as we would like it to be continues until the eleven o'clock newscast, when suddenly we are plunged into the world as it is. Here, as you know, love and virtue are not always triumphant.

* *Rules for Revolution* (to be published by Random House, New York).

In the world as it is, man moves primarily because of self-interest.

In the world as it is, the right things are usually done for the wrong reasons, and vice versa.

In the world as it is, constructive actions have been reactions to a threat.

In the world as it is, a value judgment is rarely, if ever, made on the basis of what is best. Life does not accord us this luxury. Decisions are made on the criteria of alternatives.

In the world as it is, "compromise" is not an ugly but a noble word. If the whole free way of life could be summed up in one word it would be "compromise." A free way of life is a constant conflict punctuated by compromises which then serve as a jumping-off point for further conflict, more compromises, more conflict, in the never-ending struggle toward achieving man's highest goals.

In the world as it is, what you call morality is to a significant degree a rationalization of the position you occupy in the power pattern at a particular time. If you are a *Have-Not* and want *to get,* than you are always appealing to "a higher than man-made law," since the status quo has made the laws. If you are a *Have* and are out *to keep,* then you are constantly talking about the sanctity of the law and the responsibility of gradual operation "through accepted channels."

In the world as it is, one must begin from where one is. A political idiot knows that most major issues are national, and in some cases international, in scope. They cannot be coped with on the local community level. The Back of the Yards Council at the zenith of its power could not deal with its most pressing problem of its time, the issue of widespread unemployment, until our whole economy boomed as a result of world developments. Until the people of the East and West and other parts of the country had the money to buy meat there would be unemployment in the Back of the Yards regardless of anything the Back of the Yards Council could do. This is obvious. However, it is just as clear that in order to create a national movement one must first build the parts to put together. The building of the parts is a tough, tedious, time-consuming, often monotonous and frequently frustrating job. There is no detour to avoid this means to the end of building a national movement. To organize the automobile industry each part of General Motors from Chevrolet to Cadillac, to sub-contracting plants making automobile parts from batteries to hub caps, had to be organized and then put together, and then General Motors was organized. The same process had to be followed with Chrysler and its constituent parts and then Ford and its parts, and now the bigger parts were ready to be put together and there was a nationwide automobile workers union.

The fundamental issue is how we go about building a national movement when so many of the present generation do not want to undergo the experience in time or detail of the organization of the parts, or of the local areas of organization. They want to jump right into a "national organization." Either they do not want to do the tough and tedious job of building the parts, or are incapable of it, or it is a combination of both. Creative organizers are a rarity. And so a part of the present generation takes refuge in a revolution of rhetoric and calls national meetings of fifty "state representatives" who represent no more than themselves, and one wonders at times how much of even that they do. It is an escape from the world as it is.

In the world as it is, irrationalities play a significant part. Life does not break down logically into Roman numerals I, II, and III, and sections (a), (b), and (c). It becomes tremendously important to understand, accept, and be comfortable with the irrationalities that are part of the life about us.

At this point I am reminded of a statement made

by the Israeli representative to the United Nations during the meetings on a major Near East crisis. In presenting Israel's case and pointing to the many alternatives, he commented, "I am sanguine enough to believe that we may finally come to wisdom after all other alternatives have been tried."

Let me give you an example of what I mean by some of the differences between the world as it is and the world as we would like it to be. Recently, after lecturing at Stanford University, I met a Soviet professor of political economics from the University of Leningrad. The opening of our conversation was illustrative of the definitions and outlook of those who live in the world as it is. The Russian began by asking me, "Where do you stand on communism?" I replied, "That's a bad question since the real question is, assuming both of us are operating in and thinking of the world as it is, 'Whose Communists are they—yours or ours?' If they are ours, then we are all for them. If they are yours, obviously we are against them. Communism itself is irrelevant. The issue is whether they are on our side or yours. Now, if you Russians didn't have a first mortgage on Castro, we would be talking about Cuba's right to self-determination and the fact that you couldn't have a free election until after there had been a period of education following the repression of the dictatorship of Batista. As a matter of fact, if you should start trying to push for a free election in Yugoslavia, we might even send over our Marines to prevent this kind of sabotage. The same goes if you should try to do it in Formosa." The Russian came back with, "What is your definition of a free election outside of your country?" I said, "Well, our definition of a free election in, say, Vietnam is pretty much what your definition is in your satellites—if we've got everything so set that we are going to win, then it's a free election. Otherwise, it's bloody terrorism! Isn't that your definition?" The Russian's reaction was, "Well, yes, more or less!"

I strongly suggest to you that this is not cynicism but realism. Ideologies are not very significant in themselves. The Soviet power position and its so-called ideology or rationalizations shifted drastically as the Russians moved from a *Have-Not* to a *Have* society, just as ours did when we moved from a *Have-Not* to a *Have* nation.

The younger generation must soon swing into action. Action is purposeful, deliberate, designed not as an end in itself but to generate new action in developing a program. Breathers of compromises are an essential to the pragmatic social changer. The approach of so much of the present younger generation is so fractured with "confrontations" and crises as ends in themselves, that their activities are not actions but a discharge of energy which, like a fireworks spectacle, briefly lights up the skies and then vanishes into the void.

When the young talk of revolution it becomes clear how far out of the scene one can be in refusing to begin with the world as it is. They use the word "revolution" but their goal is a miraculous divine revelation whereby people will suddenly reject old values and accept new ones or whereby they will begin living up to the "old" values such as love. The revolution becomes the resurrection or Gabriel blowing his horn.

When you ask a young activist what his goals are, he will respond by talking of a world where people will live and look up to such things as peace, equality, freedom, where they will be able to "do their thing." The expression "to do one's thing" is what the previous generations have described as "a world where every individual can realize his or her full potentiality." The fact that we have not lived by these words is one thing, but how can anyone possibly assume that the new way of life demanded by the young activists will mean that they themselves or the next generation will live in the full spirit of these words. The belief in change through revelation defies common sense.

Even the professional Christians, the ones who have really done most of the public relations on the pushing of love and peace and freedom and equality, have rarely practiced their own preachments. Usually those who have done so have been knocked off at an early age such as thirty-three, and one will never know whether they would have in time succumbed to the rewards of the system.

At various universities members of the Students for Democratic Society have asked me, "Mr. Alinsky, do you know that what you are doing is organizing the poor for the acceptance of these bourgeois, decadent, degenerate, bankrupt, materialistic, imperialistic, hawkish middle-class values of today's society?" There has been a long silence when I have responded with, "Do you know what the poor of America or, I might add, the poor of the world want? They want a bigger and fatter piece of these decadent, degenerate, bankrupt, materialistic, bourgeois values and what goes with it!"

They have assumed the kind of stance in which if the starving poor are pleading for bread and say, "Help us organize for power that we and our children may fight for bread," the modern young "revolutionary" would be compelled to respond, "Before we move I think we ought to think over some basic values: 'Do you realize that man does not live by bread alone?'" It is this kind of reaction and thinking which makes the far left appear to be infinitely more intelligible when viewed from a perspective not of the current political scene but of our space program. These political astronauts have gone beyond the "third world" and are now orbiting well into a mystical fourth world.

One must understand that these student activists as well as the hippies have with rare exception come from the middle class. It was their parents who had a fixed road to happiness by making that house out in the suburbs, the bank account, the country club, the color TV set, and two cars in the garage. If the parents got these things they would have it made. The parents are the ones who worked, followed all the signposts and got the goods for the promised good life but who, instead, now find themselves lost in Nowhere.

They are even more alienated from the scene than the poor because what they had after they got it was not the good life; they do not know where to go, they lack any compass or direction, so they founder and are frightened. The poor at least have a compass, a direction, and a purpose because, regardless of what anyone says to them, getting that bank account, that color TV, that house in the suburbs, and two cars is happiness. One can never reject these possessions unless one has experienced them, just as you cannot preach spiritual values to someone who is starving and whose idea of happiness is having enough food. It is after he achieves enough food for today and all of the tomorrows that he moves to the next stage, realizing that this has not brought him happiness. Then he is ready for, and starts demanding, other things. Until that time you can no more tell a person striving for physical survival that survival in itself will not bring him happiness any more than you can tell a drowning man that a lifeline is not more important than anything else. On the West Coast the story is told of a white hippie preaching rejection of the system and all its immoral values, and pleading for members of his audience to drop out and join the hippies. At this point a young black spoke up, "Hey, how can I drop out when I ain't never been in?"

Those student activists who refuse to be realistic are so far left that they're out of the arena. They were not even envisaged in Nikolai Lenin's *"Left-Wing" Communism, an Infantile Disorder*. If Lenin were writing about our present far-out left, his work would be titled *"Left-Wing" Communism, a Womblike Disorder*. They will divide and redivide into multiple cults of fragments in futility.

Unless the young radicals get with the scene as it is, we will see that the present disillusionment, boredom, and sense of failure will finally fertilize a rationale of, "Well, I tried to fight this system, the establishment, I tried to do something but people won't listen and this whole goddamned system has just got to collapse of its own inner moral decay. There's no sense in my demonstrating and starving, so then . . ." So then they get a job on Madison Avenue and at the ripe old age of twenty-eight are "elder statesmen" of their own fevered imaginations, ready to start reminiscing about "their radical youth."

Although they are visibly dropping out of "social action" by the age of twenty-five or twenty-eight, they were never really in. I would describe the current scene of these activist dropouts or political hippies as "Political Hippyitus." These young people are the ones who scream "Burn the system down!" "Destroy the establishment!" and when you say, "What kind of a system would you have instead?" they respond by saying, "That is not a relevant question! That question confuses the issue! The new way will arise from the ashes of the destruction of the present system." If, however, you continue to pursue the issue by asking, "Well, what kind of a system would you have— you must have some idea?" then they reply as often as not, "What we want is a classless society." Pushing this point very soon brings you to an abyss of nothingness.

Question. "What do you mean by a classless society? Do you mean something like Russia?"

Answer. "No."

Question. "Well, that sort of puzzles me, because Marxism takes the position that there are two classes —the proletariat and the bourgeois, so once you destroyed the bourgeois that only left one class, the proletariat, which meant a classless society."

Answer. "Well, there is an elite Communist Party."

Question. "Do you mean China, then?"

Answer. "No."

Question. "Cuba?"

Answer. "Well, there are some potentials—possibly."

Question. "Yes or no?"

Answer. "Well, right now I don't know, but the fact that there never has been a classless society doesn't mean that you can't have one."

Question. "I'll accept that argument—but let's see if we can't get back a little bit in this world as it is. I find it impossible to imagine a way of life in which people do not occupy political or economic administrative posts. That's why I'm confused about exactly what you mean by a classless society."

Then comes the standard run-away, escapist ploy: "You can't expect anyone past the age of twenty-five to understand."

It has been said that patriotism is the last refuge of the scoundrel. Today "youth" has become the refuge of the ignorant and confused. Lack of any knowledge, experience, or understanding of how to bring about change stems from this chronological castration. They have cut themselves off from any of the experience, knowledge, insights, understanding of the past. To them anyone past the age of twenty-five or thirty should drop dead—they have substantially revised one of George Bernard Shaw's Maxims for Revolutionists, "Every man over forty is a scoundrel," to "Every man over twenty-five . . ." They are implicit personifications of Aristotle's comment, "The young think they know everything and are confident in their assertions." They don't know that the average age of the members of the Jacobin clubs of the French Revolution was forty-two, or the similar age of the leaders of the Russian Revolution. Their "thing" will be noted as the "Revolutionaries of Rhetoric."

I have been so critical and so rough on our present young activists because to me they are the hope for the future. They are the seedlings from which will come the experienced, effective radical leaders of the next generation; the ones who will stand up, organize, lead, and fight for the good life. They are essential to the growth of a democratic society. We cannot afford another decade of a desert of dissent which followed the late Senator Joseph McCarthy's night of persecution. It was those years of fear which stifled and sterilized the radical campus crop of the early fifties and created the present generation gap in the continuum. This must not happen again. Failure of today brings disillusionment of tomorrow and the rationalization of "I fought and tried but people just don't care. Anyway the system is so rotten and decayed that it will collapse. I'll get a good job and get mine; or I'll be part of the national conferences where we can denounce the system." Worse than all this is my fear that disillusionment of these young alleged activists carries the seeds of a potential cynicism which may result in this "active" turned-on generation becoming the most turned-off and reactionary generation as they go into their thirties. This must not happen.

The refusal to accept the past is not the only reason for the ineffective activity by the present generation of activists. They have grown up in a society which is extraordinarily fragmented and reflects itself in their own fractured way of life.

The present generation is coming on stage at a time of the greatest revolution in the history of man— the technological age—computerized, cybernetic, and automated; at a time of mass media and the jet when barriers of distance and data have become shattered; when everything has been fractured and the gaps spring up everywhere: communication gaps, generation gaps, gaps between a people and their government, and most important the gap between people and the world they live in. No longer can the old defenses prevail, nor the classic cliché, "When you grow older you'll understand." They know that their parents don't understand and they wonder legitimately whether anyone understands the titanic changes of the world of today. We continue to enumerate the lines and values of the dead world of the past.

Those of my generation are largely politically senile. Senility is a relinquishment of life as it is in the here and now and the taking of refuge into the security and familiarity of the past. When life becomes too confusing, too complex, too strange, too much, then you turn away. Today our college campuses are succumbing to the same affliction of my chronological compatriots—*political senility*. The plague of senility is as widespread among the twenty-year-olds as it is among the sixty-year-olds. Instead of escaping by being fugitives into the past, they escape by being fugitives into the future. In both cases they turn from the present.

Individual personalities, or group purposes, or programs usually coalesce in response to a threat. These days we are living in a situation where much of life has become depersonalized, anonymous, and abstract, accompanied by a loss of personal identity, yet conversely, we also live in a technological age that has, for all its abstractness, also dramatically personalized a variety of issues ranging from Vietnam to civil rights and urban riots. Never before has a war been hammered home to the American people with such vivid and continuous impact. Television has daily brought Vietnam before our eyes—the wounded, the dead, and the killing. Color television has brought us the red blood of human agony. It moves you to concern and then commitment. There is no escape from the unremitting bombardment of the mass media. It breaks through the walls of anonymity and abstraction. Its danger, of course, lies in its reverse use by a dictatorial regime for brainwashing and control.

Economically we have emerged as a middle-class nation. Our poor are in the minority, so that even if we organize all the blacks, Mexican-Americans, Puerto Ricans, and Appalachian whites and create a coalition, they will still need allies for the necessary power for change. These allies can come only from organized sectors of the middle class. Politically we feel alienated, rejected, and hopeless. The chasm between the people and their political representatives has widened to a terrifying degree. In a political vacuum we become increasingly vulnerable to a seizure from the far right. We know that the Snake is there but we are as paralyzed as the Rabbit. People are not rabbits, and America must shake off this nightmare and awake again. The middle classes must be organized for action, for claiming their rights and powers of citizenship in a free society. The organization must be committed to the values of a free and open society. The middle classes must begin to participate as citizens for those ideals which give meaning and purpose to life.

Logic and faith go together as the opposite sides of the same shield. We know by our intelligence the greatness and desirability of a free and open society over all other alternatives. Logic tells us, "We'll believe it when we see it." But there is also the converse, faith. Faith, or belief in the people, tells us, *"We'll see it when we believe it."*

1969
Chicago, Illinois

About the Author

SAUL ALINSKY was born in Chicago in 1909, and educated first in the streets of that city and then in its university. Graduate work at the University of Chicago in criminology introduced him to the Capone gang, and later to Joliet State Prison, where he studied prison life.

He founded what is known today as the Alinsky ideology and Alinsky concepts of mass organization for power. His work in organizing the poor to fight for their rights as citizens has been internationally recognized. In the late 1930's he organized the Back of the Yards area in Chicago (Upton Sinclair's *Jungle*). Subsequently, through the Industrial Areas Foundation which he began in 1940, Mr. Alinsky and his staff have helped to organize communities not only in Chicago but throughout the country from the black ghetto of Rochester, New York, to the Mexican American barrios of California. Today Mr. Alinsky's organizing attention has turned to the middle class, and he and his associates have a Training Institute for organizers. Mr. Alinsky's early organizing efforts resulted in his being arrested and jailed from time to time, and it was on such occasions that he wrote most of *Reveille for Radicals*.